AF225996

SHAMELESS

My Naked Truth

Yls Taylor

Shameless My Naked Truth

Authored by YLS Taylor

Copyright: ©YLS Taylor 2024

Edited by Marcia M Publishing House Editorial Team

Cover design: Adam Brooks

Published by Marcia M Spence of Marcia M Publishing House Ltd. On

behalf of YLS Taylor, In West Bromwich, West Midlands the UNITED KINGDOM B71.

Photographs are the property of YLS Taylor other credits Womanhood Global 2016 and Pheonix Newspaper 2015

A copy of this publication is legally deposited in The British Library.

ISBN: 978 1068 641 701

www.marciampublishing.com

Be weak so I can be strong.

– GOD

Dedication

I dedicate this book to my mother, Audrey; I admire and adore the strength of the woman you are.

To my dad, Baldwin Constantine Taylor.

My circle of strong women who are ready to give up their time to hear from me. Your words of wisdom, experiences, and prayers are priceless.

To the loves of my life: Britanie and Chinia my reasons for being, they continue to make me proud. You are both my latest and greatest inspiration.

Acknowledgments

First I want to give thanks and praises to the most high. He has truly been there for me through and through. Thank you for the light. I promise I will let it shine.

I also want to say a big thank you to the Walsall Sexual Health clinic. The doctors and nurses have been so supportive and friendly.

Big thank you to Marcia M Spence, The Memoir Motivator, this book wouldn't be possible without you. The encouragement and support has been on point. The 90 Day Challenge and one to one cussing, when I wanted to give up, kept me focussed. You have encouraged me to keep going, always.

To my editor Dawn Spence and Marcia M Publishing House team, who have worked on the book. Thank you.

A big thank you to Adam Brooks for creating my book cover and my video. Thank you so much, the support and love has been felt.

Thank you to all my family, friends and loved ones who didn't cringe when I shared my story. To my daughters, thank you. Thank you, the love has been unbelievable. To the ladies who have my back no matter what or how bad of a state I get in. Thanks for the prayer and encouragement to keep going.

Thank you, Audrey Jackson, my prayer partner, my big, big support during this time.

Thank you Sean McKenzie. You have always believed in me, and always ready to support when and where you can. Love you.

Thanks to New Jerusalem for allowing me to share my story for the first time in public. Thank you Bishop Melvin Brooks and Pastor Yvonne Brooks.

Thanks to Umbrella Sexual Health Services for the support, I have received. Thank you Jara Phattey.

Table of Contents

Foreword

This is the day that the Lord has made. We shall rejoice and be glad in it.

Shameless My Naked Truth by Y.L.S Taylor, a labour of love. In fact, Y.L.S Taylor herself has been a labour of love for me ever since we met in 2012. I often refer to her as the most beautiful girl in the world or Miss Jamaica and when calling to her lovingly, I say, "Yow, gyal!" And we both laugh.

This book is a culmination of Yanique's dedication and commitment to her personal and spiritual growth. When we met while she was doing my nails, our discussions were those of inspirational people, books, and self-development. Yanique then embarked on many coaching programmes with me and others. What I loved about Yanique, as a mentee, was her total commitment to personal growth. This woman has invested even beyond her means into building herself into a better person and to achieving her goals and dreams.

I have to admit; I fell in love with Yanique. Behind the beautiful fashionista is a deep and sensitive soul who needed to address and heal from childhood trauma. We all see Yanique and assume that she is super sure of herself, however throughout our journey we uncovered her need to face her fears to be bold and to continue to be beautiful both on the inside and outside.

Shameless My Naked Truth reveals the true nature of this woman, a woman who could be me, you, or any other woman that we meet. You see, we are more than what can be seen on the outside, as humans, we make the mistake of judging a book by its cover (pardon the pun).

This memoir is a deeply profound unmasking of Yanique's truth, the truths that she had so cleverly been able to hide for many years. Yanique knew that in order to be free of shame, embarrassment, and low self-esteem she had to release this, her story. Y.L.S Taylor is a remarkable writer whose style is conversational, relatable, raw and so enjoyable to engage with. She has carefully ensured that she depicts her character and her experiences with clarity and creativity.

I commend her for yielding to the process of writing and developing a truthful and authentic memoir. It is my heart's desire for this book to reach those who are suffering with shame and those who believe they are unworthy. I suggest that all seriously consider taking a leaf out of Yanique's book and address their naked truth once and for all.

Marcia M Spence N.P.Q.I.C.L, FRSA, Director Marcia M Publishing House Ltd, Editor-in-Chief MBCC Magazine.

Introduction

My name is Yanique Latoya Simone Taylor. Born on May 24th 1979, at the Spanish Town Hospital, St Catherine Jamaica. I went to St Catherine Primary School in Spanish Town and then on to Spanish Town Secondary School. I am a true Spanish Town girl, right through and through, born and bred and stretched to the edge.

I have written this book for me, for us. This is my story, our story, my journey, our journey, my healing, our healing. I say this because, although my story is unique to me, it is not dissimilar to the life stories of millions, if not billions, of women throughout the world and the ages. It's not written to bash anyone or make anyone look bad. It's not a blame story. I am not a victim. It's my naked truth, and I am now in a place where God is shouting to me, "it's time to share those stories." Then, me looking around when I hear the shouting only to hear further, "yes, yuh mi shouting at, don't mek mi get any louder." My stomach churns with the thought of having to tell this story, my story, our story. For me to really tell this story, I had to go through being alone, the healing process, the crying, the anger, the frustrations, and, worst of all, the DEPRESSION. I had to highlight that D word because depression is no joke, and I had to learn some hard truths about myself and not only learn them, but face them too. I had to admit my vulnerabilities and know and understand that it's ok to be vulnerable. They say feel the fear and do it, anyway. Well, for me, it was facing the shame and doing it, anyway.

One day, I was faced with the question, "how is your depression? Explain what it is really like." I had to stop and really think, and once I started to explain what it looks like and feels like, I lost it. I was bawling as if I'd just heard the news of losing my children. I ended up crying for three days straight; everything came pouring out of me like a flood gate being burst open under the pressure. I couldn't stop the tears. I realised for the very first time that I really, really, really, really **needed** help. I was always angry, very angry. I thought I was angry with everyone until I had to be alone. I wasn't angry with anyone. I was angry with myself. Angry at how I could have allowed so much and put up with so much from others, I had to take responsibility for my actions, not pointing fingers and blaming everyone else but pointing at me and taking responsibility for my part, too. Understanding that people can only do what you allow them to do. I had to get help and start talking to someone, open my mouth, not only brushing the surface but getting deep and underneath, speaking my truth.

My life at this moment feels like I've lived 100 years; like I've lived so many lives and still have a hundred more to go. I sometimes ask God, sometimes in anger, "why have I been through so much, Lord and still want to live, still fighting to hold on, having a great spirit of HOPE?" I do not get why I would still fight to live to the point of writing about the things I've been through. Then I hear God say, "IT'S NOT ABOUT YOU. All of what you've been through, it's now time to heal those who are waiting on the CHOSEN one, YOU. All your life, you've heard from others, 'why can't you shut your mouth and nuh sey nutten'? Well, this time, I am telling you, don't shut yuh mouth and chat everything, free up yuh self-mi chile. A mi a yuh daddy, so nuh weapon will prosper, and any tongue that talk against you will perish inna my name Jesus."

Who Am I? I am who God sees.

The scripture I connected with that tells me who I am in Christ is **1 Peter 2: 9&10***.*

Scripture written as affirmation: The Passion Translation (TPT)

I am God's chosen treasure – priest who is a queen, a spiritual "nation" set apart as God's devoted one. He called me out of darkness to experience His light, and now He claims me as His very own. He did this so that I would broadcast His glorious wonders throughout the world. For at one time, I was not God's person, but now I am. At one time I knew nothing of God's mercy, because I hadn't received it yet, but now I am drenched with it!

You might have thought that you know me, for those who think they know me, but let's see how it goes after reading my truth, my naked truth.

ONE

ONE

My first therapy session was scary. I almost cancelled as I was so afraid of the unknown. Being from my cultural background, this was never an option or something you would resort to, as if it reached that level, it simply means you are mad or crazy. That's what they called my Dad. I was someone who grew up thinking my Dad was a madman and following everyone else and labelling him worthless. He had a mental illness, and I didn't know, as we knew nothing about what that meant. It wasn't even a word I ever heard of my whole life living in Jamaica. The word for that was either crazy or mad. I now can imagine how my Dad must have felt all his life. I cry sometimes, thinking about it, as I now felt sorry for him. He died not knowing he was loved, especially by his only child, how horrible that must have felt. I can imagine how those things would probably have caused him to get worse with his illness when he couldn't get the love and understanding from his only child. I remember when I heard of my Dad's passing; I was crying almost most of the day and couldn't understand how I was tearing up like this for a man I didn't even know. But I realised it was tears of regret and guilt. I felt ashamed that I never took the time to get to know him and actually get to understand his illness; I didn't even know what his mental illness was. That's how far from reality I was when it came to this condition of being mentally ill.

Taking this leap to have therapy showed how bad things had become and I had to decide for me or else it would probably be a different story being told now, probably a story being told by someone else. The most I heard about mental health or depression was when I started living in the UK. Hearing about it was one thing, but understanding it was on a whole different level, as most times this thing called depression isn't understood until you have experienced it. And let me say this I experienced it. I experienced it on a whole deeper level.

I remember witnessing my mom coming in from work, putting down her handbag and whatever else she had in her hands on the kitchen floor, and going straight to cooking dinner for my stepfather. Our kitchen was at the back of the house; we would enter the house from the back, so the kitchen would be the first thing you see when you enter the house. It was a small extension kitchen, much bigger than the original kitchen. Once you enter the door, the countertops, stove, and sink are to the left, and the dining area with the refrigerator is to the right. The windows were over the sink area, with those short flowery curtains, parted open with the strings and tied to the sides to create an area to look through the windows, so while washing up the dishes, you could faass on the Neighbourhood. I think my mom loved faassing because she was always washing up and peeping through the window at whatever was going on outside.

I was confused whenever I saw my mom come home from work and drop everything to start the cooking. She did not go and change off her clothes, at least, and then start cooking. This would happen every day except the weekends, as she wouldn't be at work on the weekends. My mom would cook the dinner fresh to the taste because this man had diabetes, and no salt was involved in the food cooked by my mom. She would share his food like a king, rice or hard food in one dish, meat in another and salad in the next. The table was also set for a king. To be fair, this was how it was done, but I didn't think he deserved that kind of treatment. This was really upsetting, as he was horrible to my mom, in my opinion, and I hated him to my core. My mom would do the laundry every Friday evening and Saturday morning with her bare hands, and I thought, can't he buy her a washing machine to make the washing easier for her? He did nothing in the house. He sat there as my mom served him and took care of him. From seeing all of this and how my stepfather was so ungrateful and horrible, I made a conscious decision from an early age that I never wanted to become a wife.

I remembered one night clearly because I wanted to kill him. He came home very late. It must have been around 1am on a weekend morning. I can't remember the exact day, but it was definitely a weekend day. My mom had cooked dinner for him as usual, but because it was late and he hadn't returned home from wherever he went, I think he went to the country with friends. That's another thing: he never carried my mom anywhere. My mom put the food in the fridge and went to bed, as it was late. Around 1 am, my stepfather came home, and I could hear him opening the fridge and mumbling something. Then I heard him close the fridge and make his way upstairs. He woke up my mom and started arguing with her about sharing out food for him. I cringed because I wanted to get up and push him down the stairs and say, "you share your own food. It's too late now for king treatment, you ungrateful hog!" How dare he come home this late and demand that my mom share out his food? How pathetic and petty can he be? And what burned me the most was my mom getting up out of bed and actually sharing out some food for him.

I wanted to scream fire, as this was insane and way too uncomfortable for me. This, too, solidified my decision to never become a wife, because if this is how you are treated as a wife, then no thank you, ma'am. I'm good with being the girl on the side with no responsibility for caring for no man.

Seeing how my stepfather treated my mom and spoke to her caused me to never want a committed relationship, as no man was going to treat or talk to me like that. "You mussi Bl@@%& mad!" I would say, as them times from an early age, I used to spit bad words like every two secs or as much as I could say at a time. I loved hearing myself curse as I had a way with words, and bwoy, I did swear sweet. My mom used to say, "Gyal, I don't know where you get that mouth from." It was terrible looking back now, as I never hesitated to curse and curse I would. I was passionate about putting people in their place and straightening them out.

"Me, no man can get me to wash, cook and clean for them. They can 'Get Lost.'"

You see, from early on, I didn't settle for a relationship as all I could see around me was men cheating, and it confirmed my thoughts about relationships and men when these same men would want to date me. I never dated a married man, but he had to be in a relationship with someone else because that meant he was not my responsibility. And I was dead serious. My emotions where men were concerned was cold and heartless. I would do a lot of pretending as it would feel like pressure to actually care, and not only that, but if I did care, I wouldn't dare let you know how much, only enough to keep the relationship going for a while. For the most part, I think I struggled to communicate those emotions at the time.

I wasn't open and ready for what was called love. It felt safe holding on to my feelings; this was the only way I knew how to be. It was so bad that one Valentine's Day; I remember getting my boyfriend I was dating a card with an icy mint in it (this was literally a card with mint inside the card itself.) This was to show how cold I was, and I wasn't going to spend my money and get anything expensive for him, so an icy mint was good enough with the card. At the time, that was a lot for me to be doing, so I would say he was lucky to get that. I never cared at all. Being cold-hearted felt safe and normal for me then, and for a long time, no man could chat to me. I wasn't settling for any chat from them. Don't ask me to do anything for you, as this wasn't about you. This was all about me until I got bored and ready to move on. I felt I was in control then, as I was the one who would end the relationship, and sometimes, I would end it because I could. There never had to be any specific reason. I would get bored and move on.

How my stepdad treated my mom really influenced me and how I dealt with relationships. I don't think he ever liked me. He would be difficult for no reason. He used to take the house phone off the hook in their bedroom whenever he was about to go out, and my mom would be at work. He would lock the bedroom door so I couldn't go in and put the phone back on the hook. He did it, so I couldn't use the phone downstairs as the other phone was off the hook. He had a problem with everything I did. One summer, I wanted to do a modelling and etiquette course at PULSE, a modelling agency in Jamaica.

My mom said I could do it, and then one day, all of a sudden, she came to me with rumours about me idling with the boys at the mall after school in my uniform. Anyone who knows me knows that's not true. She claimed someone had told her everything. So, because of that behaviour, which was a big lie, I wasn't allowed to do the course that summer. I was so angry; I felt like my world had ended. I really wanted to do this course; this was part of who I wanted to become (a model). I have never forgotten that summer and how deflated I felt because I felt the one thing that I really wanted so badly was in the hands of my stepfather. I remember wanting to cuss out my stepfather because it's only God could come down and tell me it wasn't him who made up the story and told my mom because he was not a nice person. He obviously knew that would have hurt me so much. He would do things like this whenever I wanted something or to do something, and my mom said no and wouldn't let up. I knew that was coming from my stepdad because my mom isn't like that; she wasn't that person, but he made her behave that way with me.

As I grew into my teenage years, my dislike for my stepfather grew stronger. I always felt like he came between the relationship with me and my mom. I felt he created that shutdown my mom had towards me, and because of him, she couldn't love on me as she should or even wanted to. I used to do my own nails, as this was something I picked up without being taught. It came naturally to me. So, I used to do my nails for school and had to hide my hands when I was in school, so instead of doing both hands, I would do my left hand only, as it was easier to hide. I am right-handed, so I would need my right hand to write with when in class, so it was impossible to hide that hand, so the left hand would be the only hand with nail extensions on; I used to do some of my friends' hands too, oh, and this too. Back then, I pierced my own ears at home, so I used to stay back from school and pierce anybody's ears who wanted it done. A few years after leaving high school, I started beauty school and continued with my passion for nails, beauty, and everything quirky. So, I would do my mom's nails while attending beauty school. She was my model to practise on.

There was this one time I did her nails, I did it while at home. As soon as my stepfather came home, I heard them arguing downstairs, and I could hear it was about her nails. So, me being me; I started down the stairs to see what was happening as I could hear movements with the furniture and immediately went into defence mode. As I was coming down the stairs, I saw him look up at me, and I heard him say to me, "a weh dis pissentail gyal ago?" That was it; as soon as he said it, I started cussing him, and we ended up in an argument with my mom in the middle trying to calm me down and telling me to stop, but it wasn't happening on my side as I decided that day that he was going to get it and get it, he did. I wasn't backing down at all. He even told me I had to leave the house, and I made it plain to him that if I had to go, she (meaning my mom) would have to go, too. I can remember I wanted to lick down this big man as in my head I was thinking, *him bright bout him waan come fight my mom because she had her nails done.*

There were times I would be leaving the house at night to go out, and because he didn't like it, he would bright himself and say things like, "If you leave at this hour, don't come back here!" to which I would always kiss my teeth and slam the door as hard as I could when going. *Feisty, him know who him a deal with?* I would think to myself, *this is not Audrey* (my mom). I think the happiest day of his life was when I left to come to the UK to live, although at first, it was only to make a visit, which turned into a lifetime visit. The only advice he gave me was to make sure I behaved myself. Looking back, this was definitely the best day of my life as I knew I wouldn't have to see or talk to him anymore because when I come back home, I won't be living with my mom and stepfather. This is what I was thinking to myself. And that's exactly what happened. I only saw that man again when I went back home five years later and my mom insisted I visit him. By then, my mom had left the marriage. So, the visit was a quick hi and bye. I didn't even go into the house. I've never spoken to him ever again after that visit.

I remember a time when I did not like my mom and would be so angry with her as I had always thought she put my stepfather before me and loved him and not me. I never felt like she defended me as she should. It was all about him. That's what it looked like for me at the time. I remember a time; I think it must have been right after my grandmother died. You see, there was a time when I lived with my grandmother. I never lived with my mom until I started secondary school. I remember seeing my mom; I think it was on one of her visits. I'm not sure exactly where we were, but I remember asking her if I could stay with her for the summer, and she said yes, I could. So, when the summer came, I remember being overly excited because all I was focused on was going to my mom's for the summer, and so when I didn't see her coming for me, I decided to pack my little bag and go to her instead because I was so determined that I wanted to spend the summer with her and she had promised me so I'm gonna go, anyway. I recall reaching my mom's, and the next thing I hear out of her mouth is, "Weh yuh a go, I didn't come for you, so why you come before I come for you?" and with that said, my mom escorted me back to the bus stop and put me back on a taxi to head back to where I was coming from. I was so broken-hearted, as all I wanted was to spend the summer with my mom. I couldn't understand at the time why my mom didn't want me around. Why, as her only child, I couldn't be with her. This was the beginning of feeling rejection from my mom throughout my life. My mom never really communicated things to me, so not much would be said, and I would then interpret her behaviour as that she didn't love me and couldn't understand why.

I got along with my stepfather's family as I went to the family house during some holidays. He had nieces and nephews living there, too, so I had that company whenever I would visit, and it was lovely; I enjoyed going there. His mom and dad were nice to me and treated me as part of the family. I remember having some good times being there for holidays or when I would go after school and some weekends.

My mom used to make my school uniform. She had mad skills, some of which I picked up from her, like crocheting. I was doing crochet from a very early age. One summer while in primary school; I used to go to the summer program at the Spanish Town library, and we had all kinds of activities going on. I entered a crochet competition and made shirt collars, which I remember winning. I admired my mom at the time, as she was so beautiful and always carried herself well. She had beautiful long hair, which she would go to the hairdresser every week and keep it looking fresh; she wears it really short these days. My mom always carried herself well, and until today, she has always taken care of herself. I guess that's where I got it from, too. I used to love the things my mom wore; I remember once I think I was in year six at primary school. My mom had some green khaki flat shoes, which I think were made of suede or leather, but I'm not sure. Now,

I was supposed to wear my uniform with black shoes. I was so obsessed with my mom's green khaki shoes that I had to wear them just once. The only way I could wear them was wearing them to school as my mom would leave before me in the mornings and I would reach home before she gets home from work, so wearing them to school would be the only time I could wear them without my mother finding out. So, there I was one morning, going to school in my mom's green khaki shoes with my sky-blue tunic, white shirt uniform and navy-blue socks. Did I care? NOPE! I held my head high that day because I felt good and didn't care how it looked or what anyone else would think. My confidence that day was sky-high. My sense of style was always different, and somehow, I had to find a way to break the rules once again, which I would do on occasion throughout my school years. I don't enjoy looking like everyone, so I must add something different, especially when it came to me having to wear a uniform.

I think that's why I hated my stepfather (I know it may sound harsh, but that was how I felt at the time), as he didn't appreciate how beautiful my mom was and should have treated her like a queen as she deserved. I had always lived with my grandmother, so when the time came for me to see my mom, I felt excited. I used to look forward to going to work with my mom during the summer holidays as a little girl. She sewed, and she worked at a factory making uniforms. I don't think there was ever a time as a child when I thought we were poor, as it didn't feel that way at all. I was an only child, so other kids at school would think I was rich because I would have most things, but this would happen because I had no one to share it with, just me myself and I. Plus, my mom had only me to buy for or pay for.

TWO

TWO

For many years, my relationship with my mom was strained, and I think because of that, I became the rebel child. I went against everything, every rule. I didn't care. My mom tried to beat me once when I was 15 or 16, and I wasn't having it. I pulled some scissors out at my mom to tell her to back off or else. I didn't have any ears, as whatever was said would go through one ear and go through the next ear. My mom and aunty would always be at my school, as I couldn't settle and just be. I had to be feisty and unruly, with no behaviour and full of back chat. I think all this behaviour got worse when my grandmother died, don't get me wrong, I would always give my grandmother talking (this means I'm always getting into trouble), not sure what it was at the time, but I couldn't keep still, and my concentration was too short, so I was always in trouble. Grandma was my everything, she was the love of my life, the one who would take me everywhere with her, because she didn't want anyone treating me bad or putting their hands on me, she was very protective of me and now she was gone; I didn't handle that very well at all. I would be the one with my grandmother going to the market on a Saturday. I knew Spanish Town Market inside and out. Everyone knew my grandmother. She was very popular. Everyone knew her as Miss Hay. I remember that market days were long, as my grandmother would stop and have conversations with everyone, and they weren't short convos. She had a big blue leather bag, and she would fill it with whatever she bought that day and carry it on her head. We would be all over Spanish Town on a Saturday as my grandmother would be up and down buying things and paying bills. She was my heartbeat, the one who would have my back all the time until I disobeyed her, and she had to beat me. But I knew I was hard of hearing. My grandmother didn't beat me for nothing. I can guarantee that I deserved it every time she punished me, as I wasn't behaving as I should. I was the child who would give pure trouble but was afraid of beatings. I was always running away from the beatings. So sometimes, I would be out of the house most of the day as I was hiding from lick. Because she couldn't catch me, my grandmother had this thing where she would wait until I was all tucked in bed and sleeping, then she would get her revenge and sort me out with the beatings she had saved up. Or she would get my aunty to try to catch me. I remember once slipping out of her hand and going under the bed. My grandmother lifted the mattress and used the broomstick to try to get to me. I'm sorry, but you have to catch me, if you can because I am not standing and taking no beatings, no way. I was that bad, my grandmother would give my primary school teacher permission to beat me. She would say, "spare the eyes." I clearly remember once. I think I was in year one or two of primary school. It was the beginning of the academic term after the summer holidays. Normally, going back to school after the summer holidays, I would have everything new: new uniforms, socks, bag, books, and lunch pan set.

Now, my lunch pan set had a thermos, but the thermos had a hole at the top, so you cannot put the thermos to your mouth to drink from it. You had to empty the drink into the cup and sip from the cup. I remember on the day while carrying me to school, my grandmother kept warning me, don't sip from the thermos; She warned me high, and she warned me low, as she knew who she was talking to and knew she had to get it into me. She kept saying it to me, "Don't drink from the thermos; throw it out into the cup and drink from the cup." I wore a sky-blue tunic along with a white shirt. The juice in the thermos was red cool aid or some kind of red juice. Hence, my grandmother kept warning me, knowing this would stain my uniform and make a mess. But being Yanique, I bet you can guess exactly what happened. As soon as I was on my lunch break, the big woman in me came out. Everything that was said was nowhere to be heard, and I, as usual, I did what I wanted. I wanted to drink straight from the thermos, so that I did, and guess what? Yes, the red juice poured out all over the front of my uniform. As soon as the juice messed up my uniform, that's when I remembered that I was told to pour into the cup and then drink.

You can imagine my grandmother's face when she picked me up from school and the aftermath I endured. My grandmother cussed me at school, while walking home from school, and when I got home, I think she was disappointed as she really explained to me why not to do it and warned me dearly, but still, it never ended that way at all. My name wouldn't be Yanique if it didn't happen the way I did it, because that was me. I remember my grandmother bringing me to visit a psychologist as my behaviours were unusual; they thought. I was always hyper and would play and talk to myself all the time, as I would get bored so easily. My concentration span was so short I was easily distracted, and to this day, I am the same. I am an only child, so I guess some of the behaviour came from being an only child. I don't know. The psychologist told my grandmother that nothing was wrong with me.

I get bored easily, so I'm always finding something to do, even if that means playing school in the yard and on the grass; the small trees were my students, and I would be out there whipping and beating them for not listening to me or misbehaving. I love my own company, even to this day. It's a pleasure spending time with me. It's so fucking funny, and I love it. I enjoy how I can totally 100% be myself when I'm alone, and I love it. As a child and teenager, this was never something that bothered me. I remember being in my room, always sitting in front of the mirror, and interviewing myself as if I had become some celebrity when I got older. This felt normal to me. I didn't think I was doing anything wrong. I would constantly talk to myself, which felt normal until everyone else made it a big deal and made it seem like I was crazy. Looking back now, I can understand how the times were, that everyone would think something was wrong with me because I always did everything differently. I was different. That was all it was. I wish my grandmother was still alive to see me at a certain age, as I know she would have understood me more than anyone else. She knew I was special, and I think now that was why she was so protective of me and carried me with her everywhere she went so as not to leave me with anyone to take advantage of me or mock me.

When my grandmother died, I was heartbroken, and I don't think I was ever the same little girl again. I saw her draw her last breath. I can remember her head in my lap. We were in the back of the car, rushing her to the hospital. By the time we pulled up in front of the hospital, I can't recall with certainty, but I believe she was already dead. I felt nothing for days. At the funeral, I didn't cry. I had big issues with crying in public, so no tears came, and I can't remember if I allowed myself to really feel the pain. It wasn't until it all ended and when I got home that night, I cried; I think it was more a bawling than crying. I let it all out when I was alone because, during that period, I could only cry when no one was around. It's been over thirty years since she left us, and I still miss her dearly. Every time I think about her, I cry with such passion; it's like I've lost her again.

I remember so much about her, how she taught me how to wash, especially white clothes, and how to put them in the sun to get that perfect white. You would soap up the whites with what we call blue soap, wrap them in clear plastic and put them directly in the sun for a few hours, then wash again and hang them on the line in the sun to get the perfect white, she taught me how to cook, clean and bake. She always made coconut drops and grater cakes when we had a class party at primary school, mostly around Christmas time. We wouldn't wear uniforms; we would dress up, so everyone would wear their best outfits to the class party. Everyone brought something from home, made by parents/guardians or someone else in the family. Those were special times for us as kids, well I know it was for me. I still to this day miss my grandma. I have times when I think about her and think about how life would have been for me if she were still alive.

I love you, Lillian Hay Duhaney. This love for you will never die. I still cry in moments when I remember you and thank God that I can still remember things about you and know that you loved me then and would still love me now. R.I.P Grandma!

THREE

THREE

Years after grandma died, 11 years to be exact, I was about 19. You see, my grandmother used to bring my cousin and me to church with her every Sunday. We grew up in church and went to church every day (literally) until I reached eight years of age because that's when my grandmother died. It was coming to the beginning of the New Year, and I wanted to go visit church as I hadn't been since my grandmother died. As it was a New Year, I wanted to start the year right, and that's what I felt would have done the trick, me attending church the first Sunday of the year.

I got up the Sunday morning and was getting ready for church. My mom kept asking me why I was so eager to go to church, and I said I hadn't been since grandma died. I felt in my spirit like I had to go, especially on the first Sunday of the year.

So, I got ready and reached church on time. As I entered the church, I didn't think anyone would remember me like that, but one person did. He was a family friend as well, and I think his job at church was ushering, which is why I would be greeted by him as soon as I went into church. I remember it was a great service and I was feeling so blessed to have made the effort and actually felt blessed by the word.

As church was over, I was heading out when I was approached by that person who remembered me. He made everyone aware that I was Lillian's granddaughter. To which everyone was like: -

"Oh wow, you have grown,"

 "What a gorgeous young lady,"

"Yuh pretty eeen,"

"A sis Duhaney granddaughter dis? My, what a way you've grown up so nice."

After the introductions, the person, and his wife invited me to dinner at their house. I accepted. They usually travel in a family bus. The family van was full that day, so I couldn't travel on the bus with everyone. The person then suggested that we go by public transport, only him and me, as the family bus couldn't hold anyone else. Instead of me travelling alone or not coming, he would travel with me on public transport. I agreed, as there wasn't anything weird about it, as it was clear to see, and everyone would expect me to come for dinner. Anyway, we travelled on the bus over to where we were supposed to be going. Everything felt safe, as he was asking questions about the family. We finally got off the bus and started walking to what I thought would be his home with his family. Instead, we were headed to his brother's house, and I realised as soon as I was at the house the brother was there, and he was someone I knew as well, as he used to attend the same church. At the time, the brother was no longer attending church, or so it seemed, based on the conversation we were having. At first, I thought nothing much about what was happening; I thought he had brought me to see the brother, knowing he would remember me, and it had been years since they would have seen me. So, everything looked pretty normal until I heard him talking to his brother in the other room and asking him to get some KFC so I could eat.

That's when the penny dropped. I suddenly became frozen, my heart beating away, and I had to calm myself. Suddenly, I didn't feel safe, and I knew danger was coming. His brother left to get the food, and he sat by me and was chit-chatting a bit. His brother returned with the food, then left for work and again, another penny dropped. I was now alone with this man. A big old dirty man. As soon as his brother left, he took my hand. I was frozen and numb by now. My head was telling me to stay calm. I don't know why, but that instinct came over me that day. My instinct said stay calm. He led me to a bedroom and put me to lie down on the bed. My body wasn't responding to what was going on. I was stiff and frightened. Then he asked me a question: "Are you a virgin?"

Without thinking about it, I said, "yes," as soon as I said this, he stopped touching me and lifted me up off the bed and told me I had to go. The relief I felt was unexplainable. You would have to be in that situation to really understand that relief. I went home that day with so many thoughts running through my head. One was I should have listened to my mom. I wasn't going to say anything to anyone because, in my head, it was my fault. I should have gone straight home. Why did I even think to go and have dinner with his family in the first place? Why did I go on the bus with him? Why couldn't I just have gone to mi yard?

I definitely wasn't going back to church because I'm now thinking, *you can't trust anyone.* This was so wrong on every level. Is this what these men in church do? Prey on young girls, young girls who could be their granddaughters. EWWWW, how sick can you be as a man? It was the creepiest moment in my life; I feel sick whenever I think about what went down that day. One question was asked and based on my answer, that would determine his actions afterwards. I was saved by the answer.

Even though nothing physically happened, I was still traumatised. I had more confirmation about men and how horrible they can be, and I now knew they couldn't be trusted at all. This was a man in the church, which made it worse for me. He's a man of God. He's meant to keep me safe. He was also a family friend, but he didn't care.

FOUR

FOUR

I had a teacher named Ms Prince. She was my year four teacher and a friend of my grandmother, and when my grandmother died, Ms Prince became a second mom to me. She really had to step up to it as my mom and I weren't getting on at all and step up she did. I was so out of control thinking about it now, and no one could get through to me. Because of her love for my grandmother and me, she was the only one I would listen to, and she took me in for a while to live with her while I was in my teenage years. It was one of the best things that could have happened in my life at the time because I also gained two sisters.

Ms Prince had two daughters, one older and one younger than me, so I was in the middle. Being an only child, this was awesome and perfect for me at the same time. I had a big sister, Ariel, and a little sister, Santanya. When I went to live with Ms Prince, Ariel was living in Canada, but as soon as she visited Jamaica and we met in person, it was all over; a bond was made for life. Even to this day, we share secrets no one can squeeze out of us, even if they tried. I love that even though I'm an only child and I love being an only child, I also feel so grateful and honoured I was given the chance to call someone my big sister, Ariel. Over the years, our bond has grown stronger.

We don't get to spend much time together in person, but when we do, it's like we were never apart. Santanya was living with Ms Prince when I was there, so we also became like big and little sisters. Time may have passed, but the bond we share continues to hold a special place in our hearts. When we reunite, the love between us flows seamlessly, as if we were never apart.

There is so much I know now that I have learned from Ms Prince. She would bake Jamaican pudding most Sundays, like sweet potato and cornmeal. This was my favourite. Even now, I have yet to taste a potato and cornmeal pudding that captures the same deliciousness as Ms Prince's. She was a woman of God, style, and grace. Her styling was on point; she was a very classy lady. She took no nonsense; she was funny and full of life; she had an enormous sense of humour. A teacher for 10 years who became a children's social worker and was very good at her job. She was passionate and loved children. She was above the rest. She would always tell everyone she had three daughters. Even when I went away to live in the UK, Ms Prince continued to see me as her third daughter, which was the same for me; she was always a mom to me. Anyone who came into my life would know of her as my mom, too. The Love was unconditional; it was like she had replaced my grandmother. The care and love was genuine. I never felt excluded from the family. I always felt like I belonged, and Ms Prince made sure of that, especially with Ariel and Santanya, who, too, embraced me as a sister.

I phoned Ms Prince one day, upset with my mother. By this time, I was living in the UK. I think this was one of the times when I returned from visiting home (Jamaica). I phoned her, crying my eyes out as my mom really upset me, and I had to vent to someone and that someone was Ms Prince. She consoled me as usual, showed that she understood how I was feeling, and helped me calm down. A few days later, she called me crying and praying at the same time, warning me to talk to my mom and not to keep malice with her. Life is too short not to be talking to my mom. Ms Prince wasn't well. She was having issues with her heart, and I remember telling my mom to go look for Ms Prince as she wasn't well and wanted some help. My mom did this and cared for Ms Prince for a while. She would be back and forth from the doctors about her heart. During these times, I would also talk to Ariel on the phone, as we were getting worried. We both lived away from her and were not able to be there to assist her and help with anything she needed, which made things worse.

Then, one day, it was early morning because I remember waking up and answering the phone; I got the call from Ariel, and I knew what she was going to say. I remember hearing her voice on the phone and praying please, please don't say it. But she did. Ms Prince had died from heart failure. WHAT!!! Ms Prince not here anymore? She was meant to live forever. There was so much more for her to see and share with us. So much of our life journey left for her to experience with us and advise us. Is this really real???

In March 2015, a new reality was created, and our lives would never be the same again. NEVER!!

It was around Easter time it happened. I was working with a local newspaper at the time. Before I went to work, I had a Speed Awareness Course to attend that morning, and I remember parking and going in to do the course. To be honest, I wasn't present at the course as I heard nothing that was said. I was totally out of it; grief and shock were upon me, and there was nothing else I could have taken in on that day. After the course, I returned to my car. I pressed the key to open the car, but guess what? The car had been left open all this time. I must have been in the course for about three hours. This was how much I was out of it because I had never left my car door open before.

I then went to work and was all over the place. The moment I walked into the office, everyone could tell that something was off, and the moment someone inquired, "What's the matter with you?" I broke down in tears and couldn't even talk as I was bawling, and words couldn't leave my mouth. I was given 10 days' leave from work to go to Jamaica for the funeral. I had to find a ticket quickly. So that same day, I was in the travel agency booking my flight to Jamaica. I had to get an emergency passport to travel as my passport was out of date, and I didn't realise it was, so before I went to Jamaica, I had to get that sorted. It felt like a lot at the time, but it was worth every moment. I remember Ariel saying, "Yan, you can't miss this. You have to be there too, so do your magic, girl." And my magic I did, and a few days after, I was on the plane to Jamaica to face the reality that it was at the time. She was really GONE!

I've mentioned my magic. My magic is reaching a point where I let go and let God take full control. I trust that He's got me on this one. When I do that, God always pours the ideas into me.

Being in Jamaica at that time felt so surreal. I literally was moving with the flow, as the whole thing didn't seem real. Ms Prince??? No way this can't be true. There's no way she's gone forever!

I think everyone in Spanish Town was there on the day of the funeral. Everyone knew Ms Prince. There was a roadblock. I think we were all in shock at the amount of things we heard Ms prince had done and people she had helped. It was mind-blowing hearing all these positive things about her. She was too amazing, and she was definitely loved by everyone. I felt proud to have been a part of her life. I felt honoured that this woman had love for me, like she had love for her own daughters.

Ms Prince. Queen, Mother, and Teacher, especially of life. I learned so much from you, and that has followed me all the way through. Thank you for that. I love you still and forever.

R.I.P Belzine Millicent Prince (Douglas)

FIVE

FIVE

At the age of 15, I lost my virginity. Actually, it was stolen, as I wasn't ready. Looking back, I can safely say I was raped. I had a so-called boyfriend, and we used to meet up sometimes at his house on the weekends or sometimes after school. This particular day was an after-school day. We were at his house and in his room, kissing up as usual, but this time he wanted more. I wasn't having it because I wasn't ready; I wanted my virginity to last forever; seriously, age 30 was my aim then to break my virginity; no, seriously, I had a plan. I would get married at age 30, lose my virginity and have four kids. Thinking back, I should have had a plan too for how not to lose my virginity until I was 30. He insisted that day we were having sex, and if it meant fighting for it, that's what he was going to do, and so he did. I couldn't escape the room. I put up a fight. I remember my uniform blouse was wet from sweat. That's how much I was fighting him off me. The worst thing about the whole scene was that after a while, I was exhausted and knew I would not get out of the room or get him to stop holding me down and trying to open my legs. Eventually, I gave up, knowing I wouldn't win the fight. All he did was lift my skirt, take my panties off and enter me and cum after a few moments. I can't even say minutes; it was a quick moment. Literally, that was it. How horrible? I remember thinking to myself, was that it? All this fighting for that? Where was the magic? All this talk about sex and how good it's meant to feel. I felt nothing but tearing and pain. This would happen every time I went there. Yes, I went back because, at the time, I never thought it was rape.

I guess I knew no better, plus I was still trying to find this magic feeling I would read about in books (the hot, steamy romance novels I used to hide and read) and the movies I saw.

This was my first ever sexual experience.

He would lift my skirt if that's what I had on at the time or drop my trousers, pull my panty down, put the condom on and enter with a few strokes; that sounds too nice, more like jooks, and then made his release, and rolled off me.

My boyfriend, had no concern about me and my wants and needs; he was only concerned about his juice flowing. So, for me, sex was nothing, as orgasm wasn't something that was meant for me, or so I thought at the time.

No special attention, nothing, zero, nada, the worst sex you could ever imagine as a young girl. I would keep on having sex with him as it's now apparent

I didn't   know   any   better.

That   relationship   reinforced my thoughts about men and now sex.

Sex became nothing because I saw it as a way to make a man cum. It's the duty of the woman to make her man cum. As long as he feels good, then it's all good.

That's how I thought. And so, for years, that's how it was. I never liked sex. I just did it because it pleased the man. I didn't get any pleasure from it, no orgasms and most time I would fake it until I became an expert at it. The first time I experienced orgasm was doing masturbation. I was talking one day with a group of girlfriends and mentioned that I had never (cum), and have always faked it with a man. To my surprise everyone was surprised and couldn't believe their ears and what I was saying. They explained to me that day how to use my middle finger and make magic by touching and rubbing my own clitoris, ooohhh I thought at the moment, while feeling like something was wrong with me. That night when I went home I couldn't wait to try, and try I did. The magic happened for me for the first time in my life. I never knew one middle finger could make your body explode like how mine did that night. When I finished I thought It was more of a shock than pleasure that I felt.

The magic never happened with anyone else, only when I did it, which was very frustrating as I couldn't understand why. That's when through reading and learning about sex and the female body. I realised sex for us women is more a mental and emotional thing. The man has to emotionally and mentally be connected to you before you can even start getting there. I had to learn these things before I started to really enjoy and appreciate that sex can be the greatest and most enjoyable thing once done right and with the right person.

Now, looking back at my first experience with sex and can openly say again I was raped, I was forced to endure something that was meant to be pleasurable, but instead it was horrible and traumatic.

The first time I had sex, I caught crabs this is the very worst part. It was so embarrassing that this is the first time I have ever mentioned it; I have never mentioned it to anyone. This was too horrible to talk about. All I can remember is after I was forced to endure such an ordeal with having sex for the first time, I went home, and while having a pee, I noticed something moving down there, what looked like little creatures with legs crawling across my pubic area, I panicked because I knew exactly what they were.

With disgust and horror, I quickly went into the shower in fear of my mom finding out and having to ask her for help and her finding out that I was having sex, plus catching CRABS! I felt disgusted! I shaved everywhere; it was like I'd given myself a Hollywood wax. I was clean of hair completely. I was clued up with my sex education, so I knew what to do to get rid of them, and that was surely the best way to do it, shave it all off; every crease and corner there was hair would be off as that's what them vile little horrible creatures survived from. And there's no way you could pick them off, as you would only make things worse. Imagine finding out not only that your daughter lost or dash wey her virginity but catch crabs too. I felt disgusted!!!

No way could anyone, especially my mom, find this out. I felt like shit. I couldn't even share this with him, as I feared he would say he caught it from me and make a scandal of me, so I said nothing and continued as if nothing had happened.

When our relationship ended, I became celibate for a few good months, could have been a year, as relationships and sex were of no interest to me because nothing about relationships and sex felt special.

After a moment of not having sex or a relationship, I met a much older man for me at the time. He could have been my dad, as that's how much older he was. I remember one day being at the hairdressers, and his woman was there getting her hair done. No one had a clue, not even her, that I was sleeping with her baby daddy. What a mix-up! He was paying the bill for the two of us. This would happen a lot as we both had the same hairdresser. We dated for a while, as this was just a thing. Plus, being young, I wasn't gonna take up a serious relationship with this older man for too long. The only thing going for him at the time was that he had plenty of money, and this girl loves to shop and go out and experience the quality things in life. That was literally it. I was spoilt for a few months, then got bored and moved on. Looking back now, I realise that most of my relationships back then were with older men. Could it be that I had daddy issues? I don't know. And they had to have money, or there was no point in us being together. I wasn't always cold-hearted in my relationships. I had a few relationships that I actually think I cared about, but very few and far between.

I came close once to having a settled relationship, or should I say a serious relationship, but as soon as I realised what was happening, the cooking and taking care of my man bit, I did a runner. Until this day, I know he must be wondering where did this girl go? Plus, in those days we didn't have mobile phones like it is now, so I went and was never found. I got scared as soon as I realised I was getting caught up in this whole wife role and decided this wasn't for me. It's not like he was horrible. The sex was ok probably could have worked on it, but anyhow, I was too busy trying to live my life; I was far from interested in settling, especially for that.

In those days, my routine of going out was like it was my job where I got paid a salary. That's how committed I was to dress up and going out four to five nights per week.

Clubbing, dance, you name it. Me and my friends were there. The first time I went to what we call back home, 'a dance', mainly outside on the street and the sound boxes strung up and ready for the night, people would come out and stand around in all kinds of styles and vibes. I think I was about 15 and was staying with one of my aunties for the summer. This was in Kingston. This was my first dance hall event, and it was a Stone Love Dance (Stone Love is the name of the sound playing. Dance hall is named after Jamaican dance halls in which popular Jamaican recordings are played by local sound systems). In those days, being at a Stone Love dance was a big deal, a party I would go out of my way not to miss. That was the beginning of me being a Stone Love fan. I even made friends with one of the selectors at the time so my friends and I could go to these Stone Love dances for free (selector is the person playing the music and talking to the crowd to hype up the party). It was pure fun. When I was not at a dance, I would be in the clubs partying and having pure fun. Going out, for me, wasn't expensive as long as I could find my way to wherever the party was; drinks were guaranteed. I was always guaranteed a drink in the club because there was always a man who would buy me one as soon as I entered. I didn't even have to ask. I've been at the bar loads of times placing my order of drinks for me and my friends, only to be told that the bill is sorted. Most of the time, wherever I was standing, the waiter would bring the drinks over all night until I left. I looked good, young, hot, sexy, and fresh.

Stage shows (with some Jamaican artists, sometimes overseas artists, performing) were the next thing. There were sound clashes (A **sound clash** is a musical competition where crew members from opposing sound systems pit their skills against each other. Sound clashes take place in a variety of venues, both indoors, and outdoors, and primarily feature reggae and dancehall music. The object is to beat or "kill" their competitors). I loved travelling around and attending these shows. I used to have friends living in the countryside of Jamaica, so I would always be away from home, staying with friends all the time. When I was in town, I'd go to town dances. When in the country, we'd go to the country dances. In those days, the vibe was nice and right.

By around the age of 15 or 16, I started smoking weed (marijuana). I wasn't a big drinker, so smoking weed became my thing. I tried cigarettes but never liked them at all; they gave me a sickly feeling all the time, and it wasn't worth smoking to seem cool, so I stuck to smoking weed and building vibes. My mom found cigarettes in my school bag once, and that didn't go down well at all. Bwoy, I don't know what it was about smoking that made me feel I was a big somebody. I would smoke weed on and off for years. I love the buzz I get and how much it helps to calm me down. It wasn't until I was an adult that my mom knew about my weed smoking; I think.

SIX

SIX

Around the age of 17, I had the opportunity to become a model. I was suddenly doing different fashion shows and photo shoots for different publications. I was a cover girl a few times, and you could open one of the popular papers in those days, and I'd be the centre spread or on the cover. I enjoyed doing the modelling, but it didn't last long as I had social anxiety. I didn't know what it was at the time. I thought it was me being too shy. I didn't do the stage appearances because of my social anxiety getting in my way and knocking my confidence. I would stick to the photo shoots because I wasn't the centre of attention then.

Going on the catwalk was daunting because I would have to be on the stage walking by myself with all eyes on me, and that, my friend, was my worst nightmare. As soon as I knew all eyes were on me, I would freeze, and my head would be all over the place. It was so bad I went to the doctor to get something to help calm me down. But that didn't work either, as I know the doctor must have given me headache pills because nothing changed. I swear, I felt worse after taking those pills the doctor prescribed. I remember coming off the stage one night as I couldn't bear the stares and comments coming at me. Being the centre of attention was never something I was ever fond of. Thinking back, I realised I never really saw myself as beautiful as everyone else saw. I never saw it. It took me years to realise that I am beautiful, not only beautiful but sexy, too. I would get comments every day of my life, and I would cringe when someone commented on my looks and how gorgeous I looked. I sometimes wonder if these daily comments caused my anxiety because all I can remember from an early age is hearing: -

"What a pretty little girl!" and, as I got older, "You're so gorgeous or beautiful."

I never felt sexy or attractive as a young lady. I would avoid going to the shops on my own because I feared the reaction from the men as they would try to touch me. Some would be bright enough to touch me on my bottom or be forceful in their approach to me. This kind of reaction used to scare me as it felt creepy because these men were big men, way older than me, but they never cared as this was the norm, and no one would really put them in their place.

I wouldn't wear fitted or sexy clothes often, even to this day. These days, if I wear something sexy, it's very rare as the attention can get too much for me. I think because I don't do this often, when I do, people are quite surprised that I have a great shape. *Yes, I can look sexy too.* But saying that, there was a time; this would be when I'd just finished high school. There was a Fete (a big school party we would have every year. This would happen in the schoolyard. It started from in the day, daytime they call it a fair and then when it got dark it was known as a fete) and I went all out sexy. I get brave sometimes, and there was a period when I wouldn't care and just went for it. I wore a long-length red sleeveless mesh dress that was slightly fitted and passed my ankle. It had a fishnet look, so you would need to wear something under it to cover up. But being me, underneath the dress, I wore a G-string with no bra. My breasts were totally bare. And I can remember feeling good about wearing this outfit. Thinking about my teenage years in school, I was brave a few times as I wouldn't wear a bra to school, as I hated wearing a bra. I would wear a vest under my school shirt with no bra. I think I was a rebellious teenager who didn't care what anyone had to say or think about me; I think I am still like that now.

My high school days were the best days of my life. Sometimes I wish I could go back to those days, even if only for one day. I was the one who would get into every kind of trouble you can think of; fighting, missing class, walking up and down the corridors when I should be in class. You name it; I was misbehaving. My mom or aunty would have to be at school all the while for something I did against the school rules. They would try to suspend me for my hairstyles as they were some big women's hairstyles, especially when I cut my hair in what we called then 'the Toni Braxton'. This was when singer Toni Braxton had a certain short haircut in the 90s, and I think every young girl would have worn the style at some point. (Google Toni Braxton 90s haircut and you will see the haircut, short fringe and all the back cut short, sometimes no hair at all in the back.) I couldn't wait until the summer holidays to do mine. I had to get mine done for school because I'm a hot girl (that's what was in my little head at the time), and I had to go against all the rules made; hey, don't forget, my name is Yanique. Plus, the style would probably be played out by summer, and I had standards. I had to rock it before the end of the summer holidays. Every teacher at school knew me or knew of me and my friends. We got in trouble, especially for always walking the corridors when we should be in class, but the school didn't expel us as we had good grades, so even though we gave problems, walked the corridors and fought every day, God made, we did our schoolwork and did it well, they couldn't touch us. So instead of getting rid of us, we would constantly be on probation, and that still didn't stop us, well, at least me, as we would hide and do the things dem again. I was always in the mix with boys at school, as they were pure fun, laughter, foolishness, and idleness, and if you know me, you know when I'm ready, I love the foolishness & idleness as it's crazy fun for me. I love having a great time, and laughing is my thing. I am the girl who loves to laugh.

I think the only thing I have ever regretted in my life was having an abortion at 17 years old. I had suddenly found myself pregnant, but how? I was on protection, but hey, nothing is 100% secure, so here I was, pregnant and with no clue what to do. I knew who the daddy was, but the awkward thing was he was living abroad, and in those days, mobile phones weren't yet a thing. I had a house phone, but unless you were home when someone called for you, you would miss out. So, communication was difficult. I don't think it's something I have ever told him because I think by the time I heard from him again; I had done the deed. He was someone I had met while he was in Jamaica for some time, and we had a brief relationship. Then, I found out when he left and went back home that I was pregnant.

My mom found out because I had a scare. I found a lump in my breast; it felt very hard, and you could see the lump. So, being worried, my mom took me to the doctor and that's where she found out I was pregnant. It was a scary time for me as what the heck would I be doing becoming a mom? I couldn't be nobody's mom, especially at age 17. So, my mom and I decided that I would have an abortion. It was arranged and the abortion was done. This is one of the worst feelings you could ever experience. The whole procedure was horrible, mentally and physically. It's a cold experience. I almost felt like I was out in the cold weather, shivering. After the ordeal, I felt a part of me taken. I felt like this was the worst decision to make ever in life. And suddenly, I had regrets about this one decision I had made. I would cry for days and felt so guilty about what I had done. I felt shame at the time. I would have never spoken about it, as it made me feel dirty and unworthy. This guilt rides with you if you don't deal with it. It can walk with you like a memory you can feel all the time. I know all these years; I hid it away and tried to forget about it, but it was still there, eating away bit by bit without me even realising it was still affecting me.

My mom used to send me to Saturday classes at school, but that wasn't to be as I would be elsewhere with my friends on a Saturday. My school was in Spanish Town St Catherine, but on Saturdays, me and my best friend at the time, would be in Kingston, a place called Dunkirk, if you know you know (this was a place where shootout could happen at any time, this could be bad men with police or bad men and bad men, firing shots at each other). Did we allow fear to take over us? No, we were just nuff and never thought twice about the consequences or what ifs. We were young, and life was there to live and live it! We did! My best friend at the time had an uncle living there. He and I hooked up. He was a nice, cute, baby-faced, bad boy. Tall enough for me to look up at. He was in his last year of school, so he was a few years older than me. But he was the kindest, funniest, most caring, cute and loving boyfriend you could ask for.

We used to catch jokes all the time and every Saturday, that's who I would miss Saturday class for. His nick name for me was 'Face'. My aunty eventually found out, as I always kept a diary. She read my diary and found out what was happening. My diary had a lock and key. Don't ask me how she opened the diary, but she did and read every last bit of it. I didn't keep a diary for years after this because of what she did. But anyhow, that didn't stop me from still visiting Mr handsome every Saturday. That's where my classes were, for a good while. Over the years me and Mr Handsome kept in touch until we eventually became great friends. He lived in the UK for a while until he returned home. We remained friends until, a few years after leaving the UK, he, unfortunately, got killed in Jamaica. I saw him a few weeks before he died, as I was back in Jamaica for a while.

I remember feeling something, but couldn't quite put my finger on it. It was like a feeling of foreboding. We had a very weird conversation, and at the time, I couldn't understand why I had this heavy feeling around him. Then I saw him randomly, like literally a few days before I got the news that he had been killed. At the time of his death, I was still in Jamaica, so I was able to attend his funeral and bid my dear friend goodbye. I think about our fun days and the jokes we shared every time. You were truly dear to me, as I know there wasn't anything you wouldn't have done for me. R.I.P., my dear friend. You'll always be missed.

I think trouble was set on me and my friends because we were always in a fight with someone. We even got warned about not fighting so we could graduate. But we were provoked and ended up in a big school fight a few months before graduation. So, none of us got to graduate. This is mad because I didn't get to graduate in primary school either, as the whole of our year six didn't graduate because they said we didn't behave ourselves.

SEVEN

SEVEN

I left high school at 16. I wasn't sure at the time what I wanted to do. I loved cooking, so my mother got me into a boarding vocational school to become a chef. This school was on the north coast, so it was associated with the hotels on the coast. I would be guaranteed to work in the all-inclusive hotels after finishing the course at the school. It was exciting for me going away from home; it was like going away to university. This would be the first time I would live away from home on my own. The first time, I had my hair shaven off completely, as I wasn't sure if I would be able to go to the hairdressers every Sunday like I did when I was home. So now that I was leaving, I did the big bald chop. It was the easiest choice for me. I wore my hair extremely short for years after that first big chop. The move was easy, as I really wanted to leave home because I didn't like my stepfather. I was to be away for a year to become a chef. But knowing me, you know it wasn't that straightforward. On my first day in class, I decided I didn't want to be a chef anymore, as there was too much theory. As far as I was concerned, I came here to learn to cook better or more professionally. What's with all this theory book work??? Words, words, words. So, I left that class and went to do hospitality, which was worse for me because that was doing waitering and housekeeping, but I stuck with it because the next thing was Front Desk; this was where you would be the first one anyone would see when they visited the hotel. You would be responsible for checking guests in and out of the hotel. That definitely wasn't me back then. So, I stayed in housekeeping and waitering. While I was there, I would visit home the last weekend of every month, at the time that seemed a long time between visits home. The boarding experience was amazing. I made new friends, who I am still friends with even to this day. But guess what? Yanique got bored after a while because there were rules, and I didn't do well with people telling me what to do. So, after a while, me and a girl I made friends with decided we were going to live off the campus. We would split the rent and expenses while living together, so we found a place near the school, which was 10 minutes away. This would allow us to go home every weekend and come and go as we liked without filling out forms or begging to go out to buy things. We wouldn't have to wait on special days to be allowed to go on the road to get essentials. This, for me, was too restrictive, and restrictions like that didn't work for me. The person I was seeing at the time paid the rent and the bills for me, as I couldn't work and attend school at the same time because I was a full-time student. I couldn't let my mom know I wasn't living on campus anymore because she would want to know how I could afford a place to rent, and I wasn't working. So, I would still go home for one weekend; the other weekends, I was with friends, going out and partying. Eventually, I left school because I wasn't doing what I really wanted to do. I went back home to discover my genuine passions. And I decided I would do what I do best next, and that was nails.

I started beauty school to do hair and nails, which was called a cosmetology school, back in those days. While doing the course, I realised I loved doing the nails but couldn't get into doing hair. It wasn't my thing, so I spoke to my tutor, who allowed me to complete my course doing nails only. This would be the start of me becoming a Nail Technician. When I left beauty school, I started doing mobile nails and would go around doing nails and making my money. This was to be the start of me becoming an entrepreneur. I tried working in a salon for someone for a while, and that didn't work well, as again, I didn't like being restricted or spoken to in a certain way, so I left and did my own thing. I would spend the next few years doing nails, making money, going out partying hard and long, and enjoying my young days until I left Jamaica to move to the UK.

I was introduced to a man by a friend; he lived in the UK at the time. We started dating, and within a few months, he bought my ticket to the UK. He talked with my mom about getting me a ticket to travel to 'hengland'. I wouldn't say I was excited as I didn't know what this experience would be like, but me, being me, I wanted to leave and experience something new and different. I loved the idea of that.

I left Jamaica in June 1999 to come to the UK. In those days, you had to have an invitation letter and prove you had a job to go back home to, as well as a few other requirements to enter the UK. I received six months to enter and stay in the UK when I first arrived. I had no hassle on arrival and came out of the airport quickly. My first experience of seeing England was daunting. Even though it was June, the time felt cold. Obviously, I wasn't used to this kind of British summer weather. I didn't like England at the time, and I'm still not quite sure why I have stayed all these years.

By the time I reached where I would be staying, the sun was out, so I felt it was okay to dress like the weather looked, but I soon learned it wasn't as it seemed at all. I went in all excited and changed off to go on the road, so I changed into shorts and a t-shirt; *it's June, it's summer, so I'm dressing for the weather*, I thought, not realising that this is 'hengland yuh in now,' I had to run back inside to change into something warm. This was now my new reality.

I was staying in Norwood, Penge Road, London when I first came to the UK. I will never forget that place, as some of my worst experiences in England started there. There was a time in the winter, my first winter, when they stole the pay-as-you-go gas meter. Because of this, we couldn't get any heating for weeks until they came and replaced it, so we lived in a cold house. I was living with a friend from Jamaica. This experience I wouldn't wish on my worst enemy. It was horrible, being inside and cold. We would bathe once a week as it was that cold, and we had to prepare MENTALLY to wash ourselves. We would boil the water in the kettle and pour it into the bathtub, which would be about 21 rounds of back and forth, boiling and pouring, which was very frustrating. Then, we would have to perk up to strip off in the cold house and get into the bath. And it didn't stop there. After soaking and enjoying the likkle bath experience, we had to emerge from the water and stand in the cold to dry off. So, you can see why it would be a once-a-week experience, because doing that every day would probably kill us, well, me at least.

I was left to my own devices to figure out how to live this England life. Big man (this was the guy who bought my ticket for me to come to England) lived with his children's mom, so I hardly saw him. It would be literally, every now and then, he would pop up. After six months, I was still staying in the UK and now living illegally. Finding a job was hard, as I would have to have proof that I was permitted to work, and I wasn't. To this day, I don't know why I chose to stay and continue to live illegally. It wasn't as if I lived a horrible life back in Jamaica. So why did I stay and endure life here? I don't know. I guess it could have been that I didn't want to give up and run home as a poor child who couldn't stand up to life's circumstances and overcome them. So, I chose to stay and fight and do whatever I needed to and make the best of it.

Within a year of being in the UK, I became pregnant with my first daughter, Britanie. I had this on and off relationship with her dad. So, when he moved to the UK, we got in touch and started seeing each other again and before I knew it; I was pregnant. I knew the moment I was pregnant with Britanie. I can't explain the connection, but I knew I was pregnant at the moment, while having sex with her dad and he ejaculated, it was as if I felt the egg connecting with the sperm. I was very sure I was pregnant. The first thing I did as soon as I could was buy a pregnancy test, and so it was. I had found myself pregnant at 20. I couldn't believe this was happening. My first thought was to have an abortion because how could I raise a child when I wasn't prepared or ready? I was scared and unsure. I broke the news to her dad, and he wasn't interested. He said he wasn't sure I was pregnant with his child.

We lived far from each other, and our relationship was long-distance. I would make a three-hour trip to visit him on the train and spend a few days, then do another three hours back home. I would mostly visit as I was sharing accommodation. I remember one day, in a public phone box, hanging up the phone on him and realising I was on my own with this one. I accepted it, and for the next nine months, I did what I had to do and prepared for the arrival of my baby. It was hard times as my papers weren't straight so I couldn't get a proper job. I was still staying with my friend when I was pregnant. The situation wasn't the best; I was sleeping in the front room on the floor. I couldn't afford a bed, as I wasn't working. How I got by is something I'm still trying to figure out. As my tummy grew, the sleeping situation got harder, and I couldn't sleep at night. I would be up all night, and then I'd be tired the following day because I was up the night before.

I started to do some odd jobs here and there. I had a friend at the time who would help as much as they could, and not long after, I saved some money to buy a bed before my baby arrived. I bought my first bed, a single bed, that's what I could afford. Britanie was born on June 24th 2000. My baby had finally arrived. It was the scariest and happiest moment in my life, a new experience that suddenly became my new reality. I was now a mother. I couldn't believe I was now responsible for another human being. She was like a miracle that was suddenly in my arms. I now had to protect and provide for this little miracle I held in my arms. After Britanie was born, her dad came round and apologised. He had some tears in his eyes, and I think he was really embarrassed about how he treated me during the pregnancy. He wanted me to move in with him, but I was still upset about how he treated me and wasn't ready to forgive and move on, so I didn't move in with him.

My friend I was staying with started a 'Pardner' (a partnership among people to save collectively), which I joined. Not long after, I had saved enough to purchase a bedroom set; this consisted of the bed, wardrobe, and chest of draws. I moved from where I was staying with my friend and rented a room in a shared flat. Me and Britanie lived there until I moved to Birmingham for good.

Her dad would send her money occasionally while still asking me to move in. After a while, he became spiteful and wouldn't send any money for her at all, trying to say that if we weren't together, he would not be sending me any money. Here we go again. This confirmed that I didn't need to move in with him because if this was how he thought, I could do better all by myself. I would not be forced to do something I wasn't ready to do, especially with someone I didn't want to be involved with sexually again. I remember it was coming to Christmas. Britanie would have been a few days from being six months. I asked him for some extra money for her, and he refused to send it for her. So, I decided there and then I would bring her with me to visit her dad. I travelled that whole day with my baby girl.

I took with me only her food. I brought nothing else for her, just her food. No extra pampers, nothing else but food. I arrived at his apartment early in the morning; he wasn't home, so I phoned him and told him I was outside his flat with his baby. By this time, the food was done, so I told him we had no food and she needed changing, and I had nothing on me to do any of that. He arrived a few minutes later with some stuff to freshen her up and food. We talked, and I thought we were on a good path until it was time for us to go. We arrived at the train station, thinking this man would hand me some money for his child. He turned to me and said he would send her some money when I got back. I was livid.

I said to him, "you expect me to travel so far with our baby only for you to send us back with the same bullshit you've been spitting in the first place? It's the same bullshit you've been keeping up and the promises you've been making why I had to decide to travel so far to get what I need for our child." I remember getting out of the car, putting Britanie down on the seat, then shutting the door, and walking off. I thought to myself, you can have her for a while and see how you get on by yourself. I remember looking back and seeing both Britanie and her dad staring at me, him in disbelief and poor Britanie looking like where are you going, mom. My heart sank. I wanted to turn back and take her, but I had to draw a big breath in and trust my state of mind. I thought to myself while walking into the train station, *how dare you, with your big celebrity lifestyle career (he was a football player and one of the Reggae Boyz who reached the World Cup in 1998), and your child is in need, but because her mom doesn't want to have sex with you anymore, you won't help?* Well, I wasn't having it, so I went on that train ride back home bawling all the way because suddenly, while on the train, I thought, *what the heck have you done, Yanique?*

At first, he wouldn't answer my calls and acted like he didn't want to return Britanie to me. So, I got legal advice and within a few weeks; he phoned to ask when I was coming to get her. At first, I was going to put up a fuss and tell him he should bring her home, but to not make life any harder, I went and picked up my baby girl. It worked because of how many things he bought her; I had to leave some things he had to bring to her after we left and went home. He would send money on the regular for her after that, but it didn't last for too long, and I couldn't be arsed anymore, so I did my thing as usual and decided to focus on me and my baby.

I had a friend who wasn't working then. She would allow me to use her name and national insurance number so I could get some decent enough work and make some money to feed and take care of my baby. I can't remember how I managed to get a babysitter and get to work.

I would say it was only me and God because I made the impossible possible without even knowing how I did it. So, it could only be God.

Life was good, challenging, but good. I was working and started to settle with a routine, me Yanique having a routine??? Yes, ma'am, I did. I was now a mom and had an extra mouth to feed and a little person to care for. I was now feeling like I could do something with myself. My paperwork was still off the grid, so I had to be careful and stay focused. I was now alone in charge of making decisions, not only for me but also for my daughter.

There was one point when I tried selling drugs. I laugh about it now because I find it so funny. I was a drug dealer for one night. Based on what I experienced that night while trying to do the hustle, I decided this wasn't for me. I slept in the back of a car. I was doing it with one of my friends who linked us with this guy we were on the road with. The danger of us sleeping on the road with this total stranger in the back of his car, I thought to myself this was no life for me, the experience of visiting a crack house and being in there selling people drugs, OMG what was I thinking??? This was awful. The next day, I was on my way back home from Reading to London. My friend I went with ended up staying in the game for a long time. I think I ended up giving her the drugs I had, and she stayed and did her thing. It wasn't for me, and I'm grateful to God that it wasn't something I pursued.

I had reached that place where I was ready to settle with my child and try to make a life for both of us. I had suddenly decided that the man had to be single in any relationship I was gonna get into. I now had a daughter and wasn't willing to live a certain life for her to witness and think it was ok to live the way I chose to live because of my traumas or experiences. So, I was ready for a change when it came to me dating or being with someone. At least, this is what I thought at the time.

ME & MY
MOTHER

ME & MY
GRANDDAD

BABY ME

ME
AGAIN

GRANDMA

YOUNGER
GRANDMA

GRANDMA ON
HER WEDDING
DAY

HIGH SCHOOL
14 OR 15 YRS

ME & MOM ON
HER WEDDING
DAY

EARLY
20S

ME BRIT
& CHIN

BRIT &
CHIN

MS
PRINCE

MS PRINCE
FUNERAL

ME & ARIEL

ME & SAN

ME & SAN
EARLY YEARS

ME @ 17 OR
18 YRS

ME @ 16 I
THINK!

BRIT & CHIN

ME @ 30

ME @ 31

DOING WHAT I
DO BEST!

ON THE
COUCH WITH
MARCIA M

I AM ALWAYS READY
FOR AN OPPORTUNITY

MAGAZINE ARTICLE

W P I
WOMEN OF POWER &
INFLUENCE

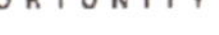

MAKEUP ARTIST
MAKEUP WORKSHOP

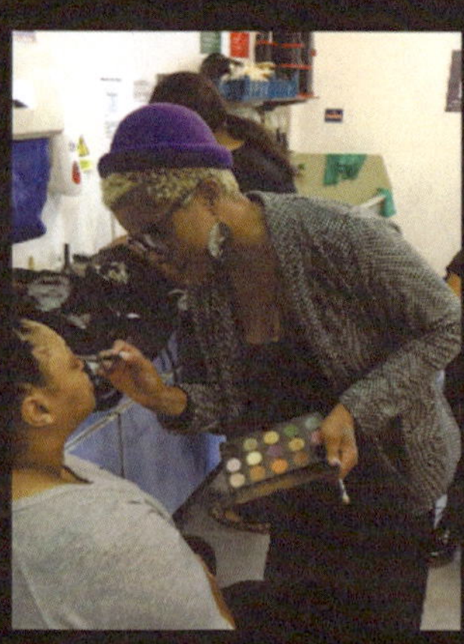

YANIQUE TAYLOR
PRESENTS
Makeup
WORKSHOPS
BY YANIQUE TAYLOR
THE ULTIMATE BEAUTY EXPERIENCE.
A SERIES OF 4 MASTER CLASSES.

MAKEUP
WORKSHOPS

MAKEUP ARTIST

FIRST TIME BECOMING AN AUTHOR
CONFIDENCE CONFIDENTIAL

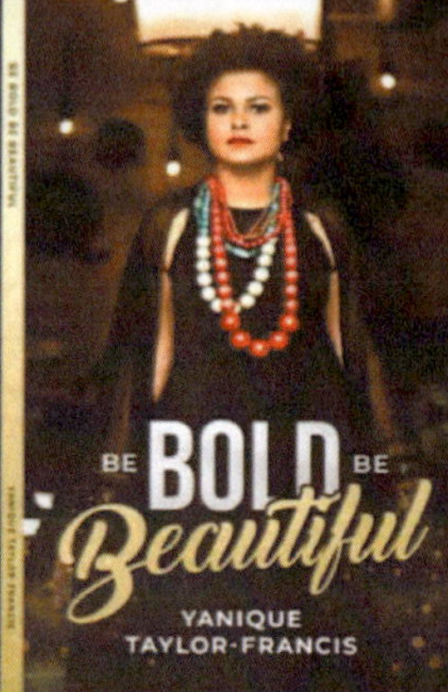

BE BOLD BE Beautiful
YANIQUE TAYLOR-FRANCIS

MY BOOK & JOURNAL
BE BOLD BE BEAUTIFUL
AND JUST DO IT!

TEACHING A VISION BOARD WORKSHOP

ART THERAPY WORKSHOP

A FEW MODELLING
PICS

ME @ 40

ME BRIT & CHIN

MOM CELEBRATING 60

ME @ 44

COMPLETING ESTHERS ACADEMY ME & MY PASTOR YVONNE BROOKS

THIS IS MY STORY, THIS IS MY SONG

EIGHT

EIGHT

My phone rang one day, and it was this person I knew from Jamaica. He lived in the same area of Jamaica I was living in before I left for the UK. So, I knew his family and his mom. He had phoned my home in Jamaica to speak to me, thinking I was still living there, so my mom gave him my number. I knew he liked me from way back because once before, in Jamaica, he had given me a lift to where I was going that day and told me he liked me. Soon after, he left the island, and we never saw each other again. You can imagine my surprise when I realised it was him on the phone. I immediately remembered how good-looking he was. He was someone I had a crush on but said nothing when I was back home. He was very attractive, had a nice height and build, carried himself well, and even smelled good, too. We started talking over the phone, and he was preparing to go back home for a visit. As soon as he was back from Jamaica, I found myself travelling on the train with another one of my friends to Birmingham, to visit and see what Birmingham was really about. It was very different from London; indeed, I got the shock of my life the first time I saw people lined up waiting for the bus. I remember asking why the people were lining up, and to my surprise and shock, the answer was that it was for the bus. This was so different from London; the place wasn't as fast and busy. But I liked it and within a few months after that first trip and a lot of discussion and planning, I moved to Birmingham with Britanie to start a new life.

We had planned for me to move to Birmingham and find a place where we could live together. This was with the father of my second daughter. We got a place together, but I noticed I was the only one moving in. He would sleep over some nights and pretend he would be working the other nights (being a road man at the time). I would see him early in the mornings. This was becoming a pattern. The man was still not moving in his stuff, so you know we had a problem because this wasn't the plan. So, being me, I came straight and asked one day, "Are you married?" to which there was no reply. I remember the Saturday morning clearly because we were on our way to The Bullring to do some meat and food shopping for the house. He didn't have to answer. His silence was a deafening yes. This was the first time I found myself raising my voice to him. The pain I felt that day in my stomach was worse than labour pain. I felt trapped, with no idea what I should do now. I ended up staying in the relationship because he gave me some bullshit and I bought it. Things got scary for me after knowing this man was married. Because he lied, I asked the questions, and he blatantly lied because he was selfish and only concerned about his feelings. I didn't trust him now, so we argued because he would lie constantly and had an excuse for it all the time. I remember thinking, *why are you putting up with this, Yanique?* But I couldn't actually answer, knowing deep down that I deserved better but didn't or couldn't actually articulate it? I felt weak most of the time. I felt betrayed and loveless. I felt used and useless, with no clue what to do because I'd never been in this situation before. How can someone care for you and, at the same time, treat you this way? I didn't see the toxic cycle being created here and how much this would end up chipping away a big part of me.

We were on our way home one night, and an argument came up. I can't remember what it was about, but all I knew was that suddenly, I felt the back of his hand hitting my face. This would be my first experience of physical abuse, and the *fights* I called it to not make it seem like I was defenceless. I would try to defend myself but who am I fooling when this man was way bigger and stronger than me? The relationship became controlling, and he had a terrible temper. He was insecure, so he would be jealous and wouldn't want me to go anywhere. He didn't like any of my friends, and if I had allowed it, he wouldn't have liked my family either. He was never happy when I went out with my friends. It caused an argument every time I went out.

This man would drop me off at work and pick me up every day. Anywhere I was going, he would be sure to be the one offering to drive me. After a while, I let myself believe it was probably because I didn't drive and he didn't want me to take public transport, because he encouraged and supported me to learn to drive and bought me a car. But obviously, when I started to drive, I don't know which was worse: him picking me up and dropping me off, or him calling me every hour, on the hour to check where I was, especially when I didn't have the kids with me. I think the only time I had the freedom to do whatever, whenever, was when I got pregnant. I would be all over the place. Yes, I got pregnant, after him trying all the time; as if his main aim was to impregnate me. Even though I was actively using birth control, I was shocked to discover that I had become pregnant.

I guess he felt safe because now I had a big belly, and no man would want me. (so, him tink), So; he thought he didn't need to watch me 24/7.

I remember one time when I was pregnant; I was very rude to him while talking on the phone, and he came home and mashed up everything in the apartment. That's how baaad his temper was. He never touched me that day, and I knew it was because I was pregnant. I told him on the phone, "Go suck yuh gyal!" now you know that's not what you tell a Jamaican man, especially if they are not into the oral business. It was messy and toxic. But after, I was there watching him clean up the mess he made. I must have been about 7-8 months pregnant. I felt trapped with nowhere to go and no one to talk to at that very moment.

There was a family friend living in Birmingham. So, we linked up and visited and saw each other on a regular. She even visited me in London before I made the move to Birmingham. She didn't like it here in the UK and planned to go back home to Jamaica for good. This presented the perfect opportunity for Britanie to visit my mom and family, considering she was a family friend, and I was still in an illegal position. This was before I got pregnant with Chin. That's exactly what happened. She went back home and carried Britanie with her to meet my family in Jamaica. Britanie was only about ten months old when she left to go to Jamaica. She came back to me right after her second birthday.

By the time she came back, I had gotten pregnant again, and her little sister Chinia had been born a few months before Britanie came back home to the UK. I became pregnant with Chinia while on the pill. Trust me, this child was meant to be here because I was determined

I wasn't having another child. Chinia arrived in this big wide world on June 30th 2002. I had created yet another miracle. I was a mother again, another little person to protect and provide for. The delivery I had was so bad it really turned me off from having another child. First, my water wouldn't break, so the nurse had to push her hand inside me to break my water. The baby was mostly in my back, the doctor said, so I couldn't lie on my back to deliver her. I had to kneel and deliver my baby, the worst position ever to be in while pushing. I thought I was having a boy and was disappointed at first when they said it was a girl, only because I had a girl and now wanted a boy. My Placenta wouldn't come out on its own when ChinChin was born, so they had to press on my stomach to get the placenta out. This had to be my last experience of this ordeal, and I made sure I didn't get pregnant ever again.

Once Britanie returned home, I felt ready again to be the mom they needed me to be. I wasn't happy after a while in the relationship with Chin's dad. By the time Chin was born, I thought we were okay; then he went and had two more babies in the same year. This was probably a year after Chin was born. Yes, he provided for his family. I never needed anything. Again, I felt trapped and controlled for all the years we were together, especially financially. It's like I woke up one day and everything was out of my control. He did everything happily because that's exactly what he wanted: to be in control, to the point where he did everything. When I say everything, I mean everything, bills and all. I did nothing but keep my man happy with sex and by being with him, like literally doing things with him only, I tried not to be controlled, and that's what caused most of the arguments.

At the same time, I was a bit of a rebel, so I would still challenge some things and answer back, which was dangerous with his temper.

Yes, I was controlled, but it was not enough for him to feel satisfied. I still would try to at least defend myself most of the time. I couldn't keep my mouth shut and leave things alone. By then, I was so angry, probably with myself for putting up with the situation and knowing I could do better, but again, I couldn't understand why I kept going with it. Was I that out of range with my self-worth? Did the money play a role? Was it cultural? Did I experience anything as a child that would result in me enduring this abuse? Not realising the emotional effect this was having on me and how this situation was still chipping away at me, taking away a part of me, a big part of me, a toxic cycle buried deep within my soul, my bones, my very being.

He would make excuses for not getting a divorce from his so-called wife. I was still illegal, but I started training for nails here in the UK and then started working in one of the popular nail shops in Birmingham. I was the only black girl working in the nail salon for many years, and everyone else was Vietnamese. They didn't know I was illegal, so I had a job there for many years, until one day I did the stupidest thing. By now, this was out of sheer frustration; I couldn't make a move to visit home or anywhere in the world. I decided to get false documents to travel and go away for my birthday. This was the year 2005. He sorted it out and we both went away, but on our way back, I was held and taken away. It was a terrifying, sad and stupid feeling, as I wasn't sure what would happen to me. I remember being asked by the immigration officer when they took the passport, where I went to school in the UK. At that moment, I knew what was happening. I said I didn't go to school here and told the truth because it was obvious they knew, and I had been caught. They never charged me for fraud, I think, because I told the truth, cooperated with them, and didn't play smart. So, because of that, I have no criminal record.

Even though I spent a night in jail, then the next day, I was transported to a detention centre. While in the detention centre, I thought to myself, *I can't do this.* So even though Chin's dad got a lawyer to deal with the case, which I was guaranteed to win, I couldn't live under those conditions. It was a little room with a small ensuite bathroom, a single bed, and a table to the side. I stayed mainly in the room until they announced food time. I couldn't eat. I wasn't used to living this way, so I decided he shouldn't bother with a lawyer to fight the case and allow them to send me home. He wasn't too keen on it, but I was determined not to stay and live this way, trying to stay in another country. Plus, I missed home by this time, and it was the perfect opportunity to finally go home. What a breath of fresh air for me when he agreed and said he would travel with me on the day to make sure I would be ok, and it wouldn't look a certain way when I landed back home. He always cared for me and ensured I got what I needed. Could I say he loved me? That's what I thought; it felt like love, but he had demons dealing with that he needed to face. I guess we both did, but we never learnt how to do it, nor did we even recognise at the time we had demons. I loved him, too, but hey, after a few licks and bad treatment, you start to question if this really is love???

Arriving in Jamaica for the first time in five years! I felt free again. I felt like I could breathe and literally feel happiness within my bones; I was home, and I was soooo happy. I never regretted getting deported as it allowed me to go home for a while and live happily, as by this time, I felt I wasn't me anymore, as I felt I couldn't be myself because myself would cause the arguments and the fights. So I slowly became someone else. And when I got home to Jamaica in May 2005, I was in total paradise. A place I always felt happy, the food, the people, the vibe. You have to be there to experience what I'm saying. I love this country of mine; I love that I'm a Jamaican. If I could hug and squeeze Jamaica itself, I would because of how in love I am with my birthplace. This is the best place God created on Earth because there is nowhere else like Jamaica or any other people like Jamaicans. When it's real, it's unconditional, yuh feel mi?

So, I was in my element when I first went back home. The kids would visit when they had the holidays. It was hard being away from them; having to speak on the phone with them when they were back in the UK was excruciatingly painful. Most nights, I would cry myself to sleep as I really missed them, and my anxiety got worse being away from them. I often panicked when I realised they weren't in Jamaica with me. Even though I was happy to be home, it was the hardest time for me being away from my children. Their dad would be in Jamaica 2-3 times a year. He wanted to make sure I was okay, KMT, or was it his fear of me being away so far? This man would call me every day, all day.

I wondered which was worse; me being away or there in the UK with him, as it was the same nightmare, only this time, he was miles away but still had this power. Again, finances played a major part. Don't get me wrong, the man provided for his family, which he loved doing because that's how he was. He took care of me and the girls, and he wanted Britanie to call him Dad, as he felt it was only fair. He took care of us. Nothing was too big for him to do for me. Whatever I wanted, I got, but it came with a price. I had to decide to deal with his demons, too, if I wanted this life.

Even though he provided everything I needed, I still wanted to feel some independence, so while living in Jamaica, I started doing nails on the veranda where I lived. It was fun at first, working from home. As soon as I announced I was doing nails from home, I got a few customers and before I knew it; the word got out, and I now had a client base. I loved the whole vibe of working from home, but it was getting too much after a while. People began to expect me to be available anytime because I worked from home. So, people would rock up at 11pm at night wanting to get their nails done. "No, ma'am, it's after hours and I have a life. Thank you."

I used to go and get my hair done at a salon. The girl who did my hair and I got talking, and I shared my concerns about working from home, to which she announced she would be getting a new shop and that if I wanted to rent a nail space, I could. Awesome, this was perfect; I would build up another client base, and it wasn't too far to travel, so my existing clients would travel to me with no problems. It caused a few issues with Mr Man at first, as he didn't like the idea at all. He was so comfy with the idea of me working from home, as I would always be at home. This working away from home idea didn't sit well with him. But it was done, and before I knew it, I started working in a salon; leaving home and going out to work felt good. I drove so it was an easy drive to work and back. I was building my client base, and life was good, when it was good.

While working at the salon, a new business had moved in at one of the empty shops upstairs. It was a Herbalife business. Herbalife is a company that sells weight loss, weight management, and health products. They had this thing set up. They called it a Nutrition club. In the nutrition club, you would go in those days, and if it was your first visit, you would be introduced to 'shake & tea'. Tea was green tea and a meal replacement shake. We were introduced, that's me and the girl who worked in the salon. We were hooked. So, the shake club is where you would get your 'shake & tea'. This would be your meal replacement. So, what would happen is, when we reached the salon in the mornings, we would go to the nutrition club and get breakfast (shake & tea), then come lunch time we would go up again and get our lunch (shake & tea). We wanted to lose weight, so we replaced two meals daily. Some people probably wanted good nutrition, so they would come for breakfast, lunch, or dinner for a 'shake & tea' to replace whichever meal of the day. The club would usually be full at lunchtime, with everyone coming in for lunch. It was a great atmosphere. Everyone shared their stories and results. We, too, were getting results, not only weight loss but also noticing the energy and the difference in our skin and the function of our bodies. It was an amazing experience, so amazing that within months, we also started our own nutrition club and were now running a salon and doing a nutrition club at the same time.

I loved it so much after another few months, and with the money I was making, I gave up the salon and focused more now on my Herbalife business. I travelled up and down the country with my team nearly every day of the week, going to different places, doing different meetings and presentation workshops. I gained so much confidence; I started teaching other people how to make money, and before I knew it; I had a team and was heading to become one of the big leaders in Herbalife. I was earning money in four different ways at the time in the business, talk about multiple streams of income. Doing Herbalife taught me so much. That's where I learnt about the 'Secret' book and movie. My first network marketing business. I learned about affirmations, vision boards, creating your day, and attracting the things and people you want in your life. I learnt so much and met so many people. It was such an incredible time of my life. I felt on top. I did Herbalife until I came back to the UK. I tried doing it for a while here, but it was so different here, and after a while, I stopped as the support wasn't the same. England has a different culture and people, so the same strategy I learned with the nutrition club in Jamaica never worked in the UK.

While living in Jamaica away from him, I had to find coping mechanisms. He didn't like it when I went out, especially when he wasn't in Jamaica. It would cause the biggest arguments when I would say I was going out, so I had to find a way to stop the constant arguments. I had to develop my lying skills and became very skilled at it. This was when I discovered how smart I really was. I had this thing I would do to pretend I was always home. We had a house phone, so I would forward any calls to my mobile phone when I was going out. So, what would happen was as soon as my mobile phone rang while I was out, I would have to run to the car and answer as if I was sleeping. If I missed the first call, I knew the second call was him calling the mobile phone number. When I answered, he would say, "How come yuh didn't answer the house phone?" I had to pretend I didn't hear it.

I would then say to him, "ring it again." However, because the house phone was forwarded to my mobile, I could still answer as if I were at the house. This would prove to him I was home, and all I had to do was pretend I was in bed. And he would feel satisfied with that, and I wouldn't hear from him again until the next day. All my friends had to know what I was doing so when my phone rang while out, they understood why I took off like that out of the club straight into the car. They had to know and understand the procedure because sometimes we would be in the car all together, and he phoned, and everyone knew they had to shut up and stop breathing, as this was crucial because if he found out, it would mess up me ever going out again. I felt like a teenager all over again. Even when I was away at my friend's, innocently spending the weekend with my friend, I would have to pretend I was still home. It worked because we had fewer arguments; he thought I was home and would not go anywhere until he returned home.

NINE

NINE

It all worked perfectly to plan until when I returned to England, and my own family member decided to get involved in my relationship, and she told him everything. She even did it in front of my face, and the lies that she made up for me to look bad were unbelievable. This was a family member I grew up with, the same family member that I sent for to come to England and was still living with me, the same family member I made sure to make arrangements for to sort out her immigration status even while I was being deported and living in Jamaica. The family member that didn't know that Mr Man didn't want to do anything to help her. I had to preach, beg, and show him why it was necessary until he agreed and sorted it. Within months, everything was set in place for everyone. I was living in Jamaica and making sure everyone's status was getting sorted. My family member went as far as to say I didn't send for her and that it was the kids' dad, the man who didn't know her at all. She only knew him when she came to live in the UK. Anything he did was because I wanted him to do it. I think my family member didn't realise that even though he had the money; I made the decisions about everything. Nothing was done until we spoke about it. She even went as far as sending him a postcard while he was visiting one year while I was still there. She wrote and thanked him for all he had done for her and was so grateful because none of her family would have done that. HUH???? I was the one doing it, not him. Am I not your family??? I didn't get it. To this day, I don't understand how someone could blatantly be so fool and make themself look so dumb and wicked to their own family member, a family member who has always looked out for them, ALWAYS, probably even more than I looked out for my own mom.

Returning from Jamaica to the house that once felt like home was a nightmare. I felt like I had walked into hell. Suddenly, my own family member was on the kid's dad's side, even after she witnessed the beatings and cheatings. I felt like I could kill her. This was horrible. Can someone hate you this much?? Your own flesh and blood, the same person you helped and cared for and ensured they were ok and on the right track. I couldn't understand; there was no way to understand what was really going on. It was that bad when I came back home, I wondered if she was having an affair with him, because what could be the reason for this behaviour, but even though he was horrible, I knew he wouldn't, but as they say, "hey, you never know."

Years after, when I did therapy, in one of my sessions, a memory came back to me. This was before my grandmother died. I remember my grandmother used to come home and examine me and ask me if that family member had hit me today. I remembered she used to beat me every day when my grandmother went to work. As soon as she knew my grandmother was coming home, she would manipulate me and be friendly and ask me not to tell my grandmother that she had beaten me yet once again. I would sometimes hear my grandmother cussing her off and telling her not to put her hands on me. It now made sense why my grandmother would always bring me everywhere with her. And I mean all the time, why I was her favourite and why she protected me so much. She knew that family member didn't like me and would abuse me. I realised then that she had been my abuser all my life. It all made sense now and explained why she would do the things she was doing. I witnessed her bully my mother all these years, putting me up against my own mom and trying to make me prefer being with her rather than my mom. She played me against my mom. It suddenly became clear. The scales started dropping off my eyes.

Things got so bad when I got back home to the UK. The abuse from the girls' dad got worse. I ended up at one point having to ring the police on him, as things were getting out of control. He would be upset about everything. It was obvious he hated me because of the level of lies that were told to him by this family member. It's so painful to go through and describe that I've decided I won't even begin to write about what really happened. We even went through a period of going to court. Things got more toxic and messy. The family member and I got into a fight, and I had to ring the police to get her out of the property, as she didn't want to leave. These were the things I had to deal with. I had come back home to a nightmare; it was a living hell. It felt like no one wanted me to come back home. I would go to bed and cry all night. I used to wake up with dried tears running down my face (depression had set in), which I wasn't aware of; this wasn't something I had ever experienced, plus it wasn't something talked about, so how was I to know what that was? I thought I was sad and cried every night, praying and falling asleep while praying. Then, I would get up the next day and face my children, my family, and people at work with a big smile on my face. And bwoy, oh bwoy, was I good at it!

I had to move quickly, or else I probably would have killed myself; I thought about it a lot of times, but as soon as the feeling came, I thought about the girls and knew this was not something I could do because they still needed me and I would not put any more curses on their lives. This one would not happen, so I had to do something and something I did. I moved into a women's refuge, and within seven weeks, I was moved into a new home with the girls. This would be the beginning of me being a single mom. A new reality hit, and now it was just me, my girls, and God.

I prayed, asking God one night, before I moved out of the refuge. I prayed I could at least feed my children. I kept having panic attacks, as I was so worried I wouldn't be able to take care of my children. This would be my first time with the two girls on my own, and I was very depressed. I didn't realise it, but I was functioning with depression. I would go to bed nearly every night, crying myself to sleep, then wake up the next day and get on with it. I was an anxious mom, which resulted in me being very strict with the girls, as there was a lot I was lacking as a mom. I would get angry easily, which resulted in me being horrible to the girls most of the time. Living alone with the girls, I carried a heavy burden of frustration, guilt, and the constant struggle to make ends meet. I didn't know how to budget. My head was all over the place; my life was all over the place. This, I think, was an awful experience for the girls. I know they were happy to go away from me at the weekends as they would have a break from my strictness with them.

I look back now and feel so weak and heartbroken because I realise now that I wasn't able to take care of them as I should and didn't even realise it. I was trying so hard to prove I could be the mom they needed that it became a total mess. Because I didn't have a clue, and instead of getting help, I just carried on.

I knew there were times when all they needed was for me to hug them and love upon them. I didn't know what that looked like. I didn't even grow up much with my mom. So, I didn't recognise I should have been doing some things. Did I endure so much abuse by then that love wasn't something I could even recognise and then deliver to them? Was I so damaged by then? I asked myself all these questions while writing today because I know now that I could have paid more attention. I could have got the therapy I needed to heal myself so I could nurture and love my children as they needed me to. But could I deliver what I didn't have or know? I didn't even realise I was damaged. I thought because I was out of the relationship; I was good. Wasn't that what happens when you leave an abusive situation? Wasn't that the healing? Did I ignore the damaged me and pretend I knew better for me was to shut up and live? Did I know and ignore it because that's how I've been thinking, to shut up and ride the waves?

The girls and I created glorious moments as well. I loved our movie nights. We would get snacks and lay on the floor and watch movies. They hated scary movies, so the nights when I said, "It's scary movie night!"

It would be a big, "No, mom!" It was funny because they were terrified of watching anything scary. I worked a lot, so those nights were special to me. I also remember that I would hide their cake and presents the night before every birthday and then surprise them in the mornings before they went to school if it was a school day. Thinking back now, they probably just acted surprised. The girls and I love going out for breakfast, as that's our favourite meal of the day.

I did very little travelling with them, as being in the beauty and nail industry, my busiest time at work was during the school holidays. But they would go away with my aunty and cousin during those holidays. At the time, I was caught up in catching the money to pay the bills. My budgeting skills were crap, and I was very reckless with saving. My money management was nonsense, to be fair. Looking back, I was too proud to ask for help. I'm not sure now what I was really trying to prove. I guess when you're used to getting everything done for you for those ten years I was with their dad, it suddenly became the hardest thing for me to do because I never had to ask before. And in my head, I thought I would get it right one day.

I look back at those days, sometimes I would stand and watch them sleeping with tears flowing down my face. I would kiss them on their foreheads and wish things would get better. I love my kids so much but didn't know how to express those feelings healthily towards them.

I would send the kids away some weekends, buy bottles of red wine, and drink myself to tears. Listen to sad songs and cry my heart out. I would get angry and cuss, then I would calm down and start to cry. Most of the time, I would find myself on the floor in the front room the next morning, as I would sometimes fall asleep while crying my night away. I was struggling then and didn't have the courage to say anything. I look back and think, *did I know I was struggling mentally?* I certainly wasn't aware it was depression, but deep down, did I know something was wrong? Who could I talk to? Who could I run to? Who could I trust to share my darkest, deepest moments? This was only me, and no one would understand, right?

My girls have done so well despite the challenges. I have always been so proud of them both. They excel every expectation. They were always top students in school, consistently achieving high grades over and beyond. Their reports would get better and better every year. They were the best and still the best to this day; they had manners and behaviour, giving no more trouble than the ordinary things kids would do. They are now in university and probably will have finished by the time this book is published. My oldest, Britanie, is studying Politics and International Relations at St Andrews in Scotland. And Chinia is studying Sociology at the London School of Economics (LSE). They are driven and focused and know exactly what they want, which is more than I can say for myself, as I'm still trying to figure out my life. I commend them. My heart is so full of admiration for them. They are still going and pulling in excellence with everything they have been through. Britanie has been on the Dean's List for academic year 2021- 2022. They both have a podcast that they manage, produce direct you name it, they do it. Chinia is a spoken word poet, she has been on a few platforms performing. They are both activists. The future looks bright for them. I pray over their lives daily, asking God to protect and guide them; I pray they really understand who God is in their lives. Who they are? I speak 1 Peter 2:9 & 10 over their lives.

The song that I love to listen to because it reminds me of them both, is the song by Teddy Pendergrass called 'You're My Latest, My Greatest Inspiration.' That is my love song to my daughters. When love is real, it is unconditional. I will always forever love you both.

TEN

TEN

My second marriage and HIV. Living and dealing with abuse on a psychological level.

It's the year 2016. It would have been 10 years since I got baptised and became a Christian (a woman of God). Ok, let me first tell you the story of my decision to get baptised and how I received the Holy Spirit. I think it was 2006. I attended what we call in Jamaica a convocation. It's like a convention, but this happens over a few days, and different services are offered throughout the day and night. I have always loved attending church. From a very young age, I can remember going to church with my cousin and my grandmother every Sunday when my grandmother was alive. She dressed me and my cousin alike every week, wearing the same outfits or dresses to church. People thought we were sisters. Attending church was something we grew up doing, and it was something I enjoyed. So, when I was invited to this convocation, I was excited to go.

The night was on fire. My church in Jamaica is apostolic, so you know it was on fire with the holy ghost speaking and noises from nearly everyone. Everyone shouting and praising God in their own way. Some people would run around the church, some would be jumping right where they are, but I can guarantee they would all be shouting, singing and praising the Lord. The atmosphere would be thick. You couldn't be there and not feel something moving within you. The power of God would move through the atmosphere. Hallelujah would be the highest praise. When the preaching finished, they called out for anyone who would love to go to the altar and receive a special prayer, and as usual, I was always convicted. I would end up at the altar to be prayed for. As I stood at the altar with nearly everyone up there with tears in their eyes and all praying at once, I heard a young man start talking to me and offering to pray with me. He started praying, and while praying, he asked if I wanted to get baptised tonight. He began to paint a picture for me, saying what if while driving home tonight, I had an accident and died without being baptised? The fear that came over me while visualising what he was saying was unexplainable. I immediately started crying because I didn't know what to do. I was torn; I felt heavy and knew deep down in my heart that I wasn't ready for God because I had done too much stuff that He wouldn't want me to be a part of His kingdom. But he kept on talking, and the more he talked, the more guilty and afraid I became, so out of fear, I was baptised that night. I cried the whole way through the baptism. Most days after that night, I would cuss and say to myself, why did you get baptised and know you weren't ready? I wasn't ready to stop having sex and partying. Most of all, I wasn't ready to give up my weed-smoking habit and bad word cussing. I have been smoking weed from the age of 15 and wasn't prepared to stop, not anytime soon. I cussed, then cried and asked God to forgive me. Then I would cuss again and again and again.

I was so angry with myself; I felt condemned. One foot in the church and the next foot out there in the world. I loved dressing up and wearing my outrageous accessories, going out and partying, drinking and smoking and cussing. Most times, my mouth was vile. But what was so funny about this sudden experience was although I was fighting and cussing myself most of the time, at the same time, I wanted more from God, and what I wanted most at that time, especially, was to receive the Holy Spirit. "I want that thing," I would say. I wanted that energy I saw everyone with, in the church, well, almost everyone. The languages I heard, I wanted to hear myself speaking in those tongues, too. I wanted it so bad I gave up wearing trousers and gave away aaaall my accessories. Now, anyone who knows me, especially back then, would probably say, "yuh really did want it, Yanique, because those things are like your lifeline." My accessories were my be-all and end-all. You know me, you know them. Yes, it was personal.

At church, they would have what is called a tarrying service. Anyone baptised recently would be expected to attend this service to receive the Holy Spirit. I would attend this service and feel completely drained and worn out at the end, and still wouldn't receive a thing. But I was so determined to get it that I would carry on. Even when I was home, I would try tarrying on my own. I attended all-night services, praying the whole night straight through until morning. It would probably start at 10 or 11pm and continue until 6am the next day. I was doing everything and giving up everything I knew possible to receive the Holy Ghost. Then, one night at night service at church one Sunday, I was at the altar as usual, tarrying away, and then suddenly, I felt in control, and I was speaking in another language; I was bawling and shouting in tongues. Hallelujah, thank you, Jesus. What? Yanique can speak in tongues? Nobody could chat to me because now I'm a real Christian. Hmm, so I thought. Because the real journey was about to start, and I was about to know what being a real Christian was really about.

So, remember at the beginning, I said it was the year 2016? Ok! I was on a journey where I wanted to get married again. I had been single for five years and back in the church for about three years after backsliding. I was fasting and praying; I was putting it out there; I was preparing myself for my hubby to be. At the time I was actively on social media. And on one of my socials, I received a message from someone; it was someone I knew from Jamaica; we went to the same primary school. At first, I remembered wanting to block this person, but I read the message properly and thought, *what a nice message to send someone.* It was a really nice message, nice enough to make me reply. I found the message and our conversation on Facebook January 2023, didn't realise it was still there. I shared the conversation and have hidden the names mentioned.

Our very first Conversation on Facebook Messenger:

Him: *"Hi, you might not know who I am. My name is .... I know you from St Catherine Primary as we were actually in the same class. It's my cousin.... who's your friend that brought you back to my attention. I've been checking you out on here for a while now, but never said anything. The thing is, I'd like to get to know you differently still. Oh, and don't worry, I'm not one of them social media weirdos. S told me you live in Birmingham somewhere; I live in Bristol myself. It would be nice to hear back from you."*

Me: *"Hey, the name rings a bell; you don't have many pictures up to look at, so I'm not sure. You ok, though?"*

Him: *"That was so long ago, so I'm not sure you will remember. Have a look at my profile picture and see if you can figure it out."*

Me: *"I did, but it's not a full face, so I can't see properly."*

He sent a full-face picture.

Me: *"Ok, your face looks familiar, but I guess it will come back to me. Ok, so that means you knew a teacher called Miss P from St Catherine Primary?"*

Him: *"I'm not sure, but I remember a girl called MT and a few other people. You know MT, right?"*

The conversation flowed with us getting to know each other and seeing who we both remembered from our primary school days.

After a few weeks of talking on the social platform, we exchanged numbers. Then, we met in person for the first time. He travelled down from Bristol, and we met at the McDonald's in front of the West Bromwich Albion football ground. We only met in the car park, then he followed behind me to West Brom town centre. It was only meant to be a quick trip, so we only needed to have a drink, but when we met, I guessed we looked alright to each other, so we decided to grab something to eat as well. It was nice; we had a good chat, and he seemed nervous but not too nervous. The night ended nicely, and we said our goodbyes for the night.

After our first meeting, He would travel down regularly, and we would meet up and go out. Sometimes, he would rent a hotel and stay for the weekend, leaving early Monday morning and going straight to work. He was very nice and showed interest in what I did. We would have long conversations about what we both wanted and share our interest in things we liked, like music, cooking, travelling, etc. He would send me gifts through the post and surprise me; he would always take me out when he came down for the weekend, and we would be at church together. He even mentioned he would get baptised again as he had backslid and wasn't happy about the life he was living. He said exactly what I wanted to hear every time and did exactly what I wanted. I remember fasting sometimes and receiving a few confirmations about us getting married, by some little things he would say or do. He treated me like a lady, pretending to spoil me.

There were a few red flags, I must admit now, but at the time, I didn't understand these kinds of red flags. I'd never encountered them before. Like one, for example. He came down one day in our very first dating stage. This would probably be our third or fourth date. I remember us sitting at the table across from each other, and suddenly, he reached over to whisper something to me. He whispered, "I can smell your breath." I was instantly shamed, embarrassed, and confused as to why he would say that to me, to someone you just started dating. Then he quickly asked, "Are you upset?"

I replied, "No," as I wasn't sure what to say. In all my 36 years of being on the Earth, no one has ever told me my breath stunk or had any issues with my breath. So, this was new and strange to me at the same time.

He said, "Good, because I thought you would have been upset and someone I couldn't say things to," *huh,* I thought to myself. *Is this really happening?* I started thinking, *is he that honest with me, and is everyone else playing the hypocrite around me? Is it that he can feel so confident and comfortable around me he feels like he can be honest with me?* I was confused. As soon as he said it, he dismissed it, and we never spoke about it again. I suddenly became aware of my breath, like no one should have to be aware of, as this was over the top, as I wasn't someone who carried bad breath. Don't get me wrong, everyone's breath smells from time to time as we all are humans. But when someone tells you your breath stinks, especially someone who's meant to like you, you think it's awful and pay too much attention to something that's not even true. Talk about playing mind games!! This was one of the red flags I would later learn was the beginning of a psychologically abusive relationship.

We got married six months after meeting each other. Yes, we met, then quickly decided to get married.

Leading up to us getting married, we discussed having more children. At the time, this was a fantastic thing, as we both had two girls from previous relationships, and this would be the opportunity for us to try to get the boy. This was something the girls were excited about, too. So, with all this discussion, I decided to take out my implant, which is a contraceptive placed in my arm. On the day of the procedure, the doctor doing asked me if I wanted to do a blood test. I jumped at the opportunity because this was something I would always be doing, as I love to know what's happening with my body. This was perfect as I was about to start a new relationship, and it's good to come fresh and know exactly what's going on. So, I left that walk-in centre feeling positive and ready for my future.

Two weeks had now passed since I had my blood test. I received a phone call early one morning while getting ready for work. It was from the clinic; it was about my test result. I remember the woman on the line saying I had to come in today as it was of the utmost importance. I went in right away. I was puzzled as she kept saying she couldn't talk over the phone, so please come in asap. Again, I was feeling confused and now worried, thinking, *what the heck could this be?* Anyway, I went to the clinic. I remember the nurse taking me into a room, asking me to sit, then turning to me and saying, "Sorry to have to say this, Miss Taylor, but the results have come back, and you are HIV positive."

"WHAT!" I blurted out. Then she started to talk again, to which I asked, "Are you sure?"

She answered, "Yes."

She carried on talking. By now everything around me was muted, and I heard nothing she was saying. It was like being in the movies where everything stops, and it was me and my mind. When I finally came back round, I heard her asking me if I had a partner and am I ok to tell them or would I need her to tell him. I said yes to her calling him and telling him.

Because it's mandatory, he also had to take a test, to confirm that he was clear. While he waited for the results, this was to be one of my worse moments with him. Even though he said he would still marry me because he loved me, he made me feel like shit at the same time because of how he behaved and made the whole situation about himself. He kept saying things like, he's gonna have to be taking medication for life, how is he gonna tell his family, he made the whole situation about him. It was so bad I kept praying to God that he would get his result soon. This was another red flag, more like a red sheet. But as I have stated before, this situation was new to me, so I didn't completely understand what I was going through, even at this stage. His results came back negative, and suddenly, the rain eased!

Imagine someone still professing their love and saying he will still marry me even though he'd learnt that I am HIV positive. I was in a very vulnerable place by now. Fear, shame, and embarrassment all came showering down on me. I was stripped of any confidence I had. But he still wanted me, not only wanted me but also wanted to marry me. I was feeling lost and dirty at the same time. I was living a new reality. A reality that wasn't a part of the plan, in any shape or form. Where did this come from? How could you have allowed this, Yanique? You have always been so careful, so how could this have happened? HIV positive! Wow, is this for real? Am I being punished? So many questions. Where are the answers?

The first person to know about my diagnosis after my hubby-to-be was Marcia; she has been so much to me, a dear friend, coach, publisher and even like a mother to me. Well, everywhere we went, people would think I was her daughter. We always joke and say Marcia had me at 11 years old and had to leave me in Jamaica with Audrey (my mom, lol) to look after me because she would have been too young, and it was an embarrassment for the family, and then years later, I came to the UK, so really, I'm her eldest child nobody knew about. I phoned Marcia as soon as I was out of the clinic and in my car. I had to call someone, and that someone was her; she was someone I see often; we had a special relationship, an open, and honest friendship, one without judgment. This was something for me. This thing was shameful and embarrassing and brought a lot of fear. I was mentally mashed. I didn't know what to do; I was totally lost and out of it. To this day, I'm not sure how I've survived all this time. The next person after Marcia to know was another dear friend to me, someone I knew would not judge. We too, shared a remarkable bond, an authentic and truthful companionship. My dear, sweet friend Laura, we hadn't known each other that long at the time, but Laura has always been the person with whom I had that special connection and love. She was so understanding and very open to talk about it. I would share with other people around me as the years went by, as I got more confident and knew and understood my status, getting more educated and aware about HIV.

As I've stated, we married within six months of meeting. He was living and working away from Birmingham, so I would make all the arrangements and confirm booking dates as we were to get married in Birmingham. There were times we would have arguments, but again, I put it down to us being stressed about my current situation living with HIV, as this was a lot for anyone to deal with. This was a lifetime decision. Something that would be around us as long as we were with each other. So again, another red flag was dismissed. I was so vulnerable I couldn't see what was really happening. It didn't feel comfortable, but I wasn't familiar with this kind of narcissistic behaviour, so I honestly didn't know how to deal with it. And to be honest, the things that were happening were very embarrassing for me because I'm a woman who doesn't stand for rubbish, so how could this be happening to me? It happened because I wasn't aware of the signs.

We said, "I Do," to each other on September 10th 2016. It was a very small wedding. 25 guests, including us. It was small because the marriage was quick, so finances weren't the strongest, and this wasn't even in any of our plans a year ago. So, planning a big wedding wasn't possible for us at the time and based on the circumstances. I really felt happy about us getting married. I genuinely thought we were good to go. There were some positive moments between the red flags, and there were more positive moments at the time of our getting married than red flags, and none of us was perfect.

He moved down to Birmingham a few days after we got married, right before we went to Jamaica on our honeymoon.

The trip to Jamaica revealed a lot more about him. His nasty little temper came through on our honeymoon. He has this thing where he would transform into a two-year-old and have a tantrum. The temper came, and he would storm off as if he was running away. I can't even explain it properly as it's one of the most unbelievable behaviours I have ever witnessed in my lifetime. I never knew a big man could behave like that. I suddenly realised one day while on our honeymoon that I made a mistake marrying this man. Can you believe this? The mind games were intense and got worse as soon as we were away in Jamaica.

I didn't enjoy my honeymoon as I should have. I felt abandoned. I felt like I couldn't be myself and enjoy my trip back home, as I'm used to doing. It was that bad, I purposefully chose to not remember my honeymoon because it was so far from that.

When we returned from Jamaica, everything got worse, and it felt worse, as things were so cheesy and petty. He was constantly playing mind games after mind games. It was draining; I got frustrated because his actions made little sense to me, and I didn't know what I was dealing with. I knew it didn't feel right, but I couldn't understand what was happening. I would always be excited and happy around him, trying to build intimacy, always trying to kiss and cuddle up to him. He would push me away or move his face when I tried to kiss him. I tried to kiss him on his forehead one morning, and he moved his face and said he didn't like morning breath.

I would get up early with him as he would get up to go to work at 5 am. I was excited to see him off to work and would try to kiss him, but he would reject me, push me off and sometimes refuse to kiss me. I couldn't understand why he was behaving like this.

No one believed me when I would talk about it, as it sounded made up. And because everyone knows I'm very confrontational, everyone thought I was the problem. Most of the time, it seemed as if it was me, but then I would tell myself it's not me as I know what I'm witnessing, what I'm hearing, and how it's making me feel. Even when I heard myself talking about what he'd done, it sounded insane and as if it was made up.

He wouldn't come to church with me as he said I only wanted to show-off that I had a husband. I would say to him, "Yuh fucking ediat, a who mi fi show off?" There's nothing wrong with wanting to show off my husband. I remember I would be screaming at him and saying things like, "What the fuck? What you mean, yuh not coming?" I couldn't believe someone could be so cold. No empathy, no feeling, nothing at all. He didn't care. He refused to go for no reason at all. All this rejection. But why?

But the way he would look at me and say it was like he scorned me. Nearly every Sunday morning, we would argue before I would go to church. I found myself making excuses when I went to church whenever anyone would ask for him. It was so embarrassing. Most Sunday mornings, I would feel weak and discouraged. I felt like I was putting on this face, and deep down, I was dying behind my smiles and hellos. After a while, I had to stop asking him, as I realised he was being spiteful and that this was part of his plan.

We would make plans to go out to an event, and on the day of the event, he would say he didn't want to go again. When I asked why, he would say no reason, he didn't want to go again. We would end up arguing. His plan was to have me change my mind or feel too embarrassed to go without him, but I wasn't having it and would still attend the event and make up an excuse for him. I would always make up excuses for him at first, but after a while, I would stop and say he was not coming. His plan was to make me feel so embarrassed I wouldn't bother to go anywhere, as he knew how important it was to me. Most of the events were paid events, so money would be squandered as, in the end, only one person would go. I felt like shit nearly every day in my marriage. I would constantly ask myself, "why would someone purposefully behave like this?" I would think, *what the fuck and how the fuck??*

He would be cold and emotionless when he did anything wrong. Sometimes, it was as if I was talking to the wall, as no response would come from him, and it seemed as if he didn't give a damn.

This behaviour would happen every day, and things would get worse and more intense. Most days, I felt like killing him and just get it over and done with. I would imagine stabbing him in the neck. When we had arguments, I would put my hands on him. Suddenly, I was becoming the abuser. And when I realised where I was heading, I had to stop; I had to stop letting him trigger me, triggering me to the point of trying to beat him up. I would get that angry. It was unbelievable to me.

Two years into the marriage, I started to write my first book. After getting advice from my publisher, who I have already said was like a mother to me. She told me I should write a book. *"Me write a book?"*

I would ask myself. She had written and self-published her book and was planning to start her own publishing house as people were now interested in her helping them to publish their books. She would encourage me to write. I didn't want to write my memoir at the time as I was nowhere ready to put my life out there, so I would think, *what should I write about?* Or even think, *can I even write?* But through all of the head talks, I ended up writing my first book on confidence. *Be Bold, Be Beautiful and just do it!*

It made sense, as I have always struggled with my confidence. I have been in the beauty and fashion industry for years and have mostly worked with women, making them look beautiful, but the main thing I noticed we all had in common was no matter how we appeared confident and looked beautiful, it was only a cover-up as most of us as women struggle with our confidence, at least in some areas of our lives.

So, on May 21 2018 my first book was published, and I was now a published author. Wow, "WHAT!" this is insane. Yanique is now an author. No one would ever believe this. Not even I believed it. It seemed so surreal. I never knew what to expect as I've never done this before. The attention started, and the thing that has always piqued my anxiety was having attention on me. And with publishing a book, that's exactly what happened; all eyes were on me now and this wasn't something I could deal with at all. So, when my book first came out, I completely shut down. I couldn't face the crowd; it was too much for me. I didn't want to have a book launch.

I remember thinking, why would anyone want to buy and read my book? Who do I think I am? I thought, why did you even bother to write this book? *You're only setting up yourself to be judged and laughed at, you ediat,* I would think at times. But I was encouraged by my publisher, who was also my friend, to do my book launch. She always reminded me of how great my book was. She would quote the title to me and encourage me to be bold and beautiful and just do it, get out there and show people how awesome I am and how great my book is.

I eventually had a book launch four months after I published it. Normally, a book launch happens straight after most authors get published. Mine was four months later because of my anxiety.

The book launch was a success, and the support I received was amazing, which helped me feel much better and feel like this is ok. I like how it makes me feel; I felt I had written something of value, and people valued it, too. The feedback and reviews from everyone were positive and encouraging. I think for the first time, I didn't feel like an ediat, but I could inspire others as well.

The whole experience of becoming a published author has been amazing. I had some incredible opportunities and exposure, which was exactly what I needed. Don't get me wrong, I have always been exposed and doing my thing, but this was completely different.

With all this happening, I still had to deal with my husband, always making everything about him. He tried to sabotage my book launch, getting upset because I chose to have it on a Sunday, and I know he's got work the Monday morning. Even after the book launch, there wasn't any 'congratulations babe,' or 'well done. I'm proud of you.' The man didn't even think of getting his wife some flowers to show how proud he was of her. Nope, instead, he chose to still argue after the launch and on our way home about me having it on the Sunday when I knew he had work early in the morning. This caused a big quarrel because I couldn't believe what I was hearing and because he really had the audacity to talk about it after such a successful launch. The disagreement reached as far as him holding his head and screaming, "Me nuh like yuh!" at the top of his voice.

"Huh? You don't like me?" I said, looking in shock as I couldn't believe what I was witnessing, and I couldn't believe the depth of anger that was spewing from him. It was an incredible sight. I never knew someone could really rip someone else apart like that, not just someone but your wife, who you claim to love and care for. So, even after all the success from the launch, I didn't really get to enjoy and soak it all in because my husband was jealous and wasn't enjoying my success at all. *How sad can you be?* I thought to myself, I almost felt sorry for him not having any joy for me as it felt miserable, dark, and humiliating for me.

I remember shaking my head and thinking, this marriage isn't going anywhere. Look what I have for a husband, a fucking broken-down kid who hasn't moved on from his childhood pain, still walking around with all this emotional baggage and destroying others on his path. This was some deep shit, and deeper shit kept coming. I literally felt like I was being sucked by a vampire. My body felt drained, and if it wasn't for the grace of God, I probably would have jumped in front of a train one day as I would have to make sure I was dead on the spot, because this treatment that I was experiencing was worse than death. No one should have to be going through this. I wouldn't wish this kind of treatment on my enemy because no one deserves this from someone else. When we got back from our so-called honeymoon, we were arguing, and I said to him, "this is not the man I married. Can you please give back the man I married?" because this wasn't him at all. He had completely changed, and it definitely was for the worse.

The following year, 2019, would be the year when my mom became 60, and my husband and I would be 40 years old. I wanted to go to Jamaica to celebrate my mom's 60th. Her birthday was in January and so was my husbands. So, it made sense when I thought about it to buy his ticket to Jamaica, and we could celebrate his 40th and my mom's 60th. I paid for the tickets and started preparing for us to go and plan my mom's 60th party. When I told him I had bought the tickets to go to Jamaica, he sounded surprised and in disbelief, as if it was a shock I had bought him a ticket. I guess because it wasn't something he would have done.

While all this planning was going on and I was feeling excited about everything, I got this phone call one day from a friend who was sharing with me something her husband did. She found out from going through his phone. I was shocked by this news as I never thought her husband could have done what he had done. So, it got me thinking, and when I reached home that night, I searched my husband's phone and found what I wasn't looking for. I got home that night; he was asleep with the phone on his chest. He's always on YouTube, so even though he has grid locks on his phone, I could easily search it as it was open that night. Being on YouTube without a subscription means your phone must stay unlocked, as once you lock the phone, the music or whatever you are listening to will stop. So, I came home to find him lying on his back, phone on his chest, open listening to YouTube. I thought, *yes, this is the perfect opportunity*, so I took my chance. I sorted myself out for bed and quietly lay beside him, trying not to disturb him.

I remember going into his WhatsApp first and seeing a message that he sent to someone telling them he's going to Jamaica in January, and it would be great if they could meet with him there. This person was in Canada, and my mouth fell open as I realised this was another woman. By now, I'm fuming. I scrolled down to see what other conversations he had been having with this woman.

I scrolled down and realised that seven months into our marriage, he was having this conversation with this woman, telling her how pretty she is, as she was sending him pictures of herself, telling her he wished they could be together, then he said, 'oh I still have those pictures you sent me from ages ago,'

She replied, 'What pictures?' and he sent one of the smirky emojis. She then replied, 'Yuh too lie!'

Then he said, 'No, I can prove it,' and then sent her a picture of her vagina, which she supposedly sent him a while back. He went on to tell her what and what he wanted to be doing to her vagina, and then she asked if he wasn't afraid that someone would see the pictures. He said no, as he had the pictures locked away on his phone. By now, I wanted to stab him in the neck in his sleep and end it all. I was bunning up. *This fucka was a real fucka,* I thought to myself while still reading.

This situation suddenly brought up a lot of stuff I was confused about, like how he never really posted my picture or a picture of us together ever since we'd been together on his socials, especially WhatsApp. It all made sense now why, as he had someone on his phone, he still had feelings for and didn't want her to know he'd got married. I couldn't believe he brought this into the marriage. This conversation was seven months after we got married. Three years into his marriage, he still wanted to meet with this person while on holiday with his wife, with the ticket his wife bought for him to celebrate his 40th birthday in Jamaica. Wow, what a piece of renkness KMT!

I got MAAAAD and was fuming. I could have blown fire and bun him up. I saved the girl's number, then messaged her and sent her a picture of us on our wedding day as, based on their conversation, I realised she didn't know he was married. Then I went in on her with the bad words. I even went as low as to describe her vagina in a terrible way, and if you know me, you know it was bad. All this time, while I was cussing the WITCH, my ediat of a husband was still sleeping. When I'd had enough of her, I then woke him up with the phone and the picture of her vagina and asked, "What the fuck is this?" He kept rubbing his eyes, pretending that he was still trying to wake up; you know them ones.

Then, when he finally came to, he only kissed his teeth and uttered the classic phrase, "Why yuh behaving like that, and why yuh searching mi phone?"

My temper flew through the roof, and I started to hit him. He wasn't fighting back, which made it worse because I wanted a fight. The Spanish Town in me came out that night, Coronation Market, and Spanish Town Market had nothing over me that night. All Christianity went straight through the roof, poof! I felt so ashamed of my behaviour after, but in that moment, I didn't care. I wanted to bite him in his neck and rip his neck apart, but God! I remember sitting on the stairs with my bare breasts out and screaming my head off. I felt like I was going to lose it. How dare this man treat me this way and then act like he did nothing wrong? He wasn't showing any emotions or acting as if he was sorry.

I can't even remember how we went to sleep that night, as I can't imagine now how he could have slept in the house, considering how I was behaving.

This situation made everything about the marriage fake. Suddenly, nothing was real anymore. I was angry; I was broken; I was confused; I was tired. He wouldn't apologise, as he claimed it wasn't cheating because they didn't have sex. This was the BS I was dealing with, BS on a whole other level. Even when his mother told him to apologise to his wife, he refused and until this day he has never apologised, and this is no joke. I kid you not.

The Jamaican holiday was great. My mom had a beautiful party, and she had a great time celebrating with family and friends. We had the party outside in the streets; I love Jamaica. That scene was a total vibe. Tables and chairs were put out in the street, a little tent was there for the person playing the music. We had help from people, someone cooked the curry goat, someone did the punch, another person did this, another person did that. It was so amazing as the only thing I did was go order and get the cake. Everyone else pitched in and I would pay who needed to get paid. I didn't even have to worry about going shopping for the ingredients, as people were so willing and ready to help. Friends and family came to celebrate with my mom. It was beautiful to see the love from everyone. I was so happy I made the effort because it was worth every bit. The food tasted good. The vibes *was real* that night. We all had a fantastic time.

I kept my cool with my husband on the holiday as this was my mom's moment, and I didn't want to spoil it for her, so kept things down until we returned to the UK. Still no apology, and things were getting worse and worse. By this time, I was seeking advice. I was praying and fasting, reading books and taking it straight to God, as this was too big for me to handle. I reached a point where I wanted out of the marriage, but I was encouraged to try to make it work. Which I did. He wasn't interested at all; he refused to do counselling; he wasn't having it, so I decided to do it on my own, but after a while, it was too draining as one hand cannot clap, and I was definitely clapping alone, it was only me fighting for us, and it was a losing battle all the way.

Remember, I said before that we both were 40 that same year. So, when we came back from Jamaica, my 40th birthday was now coming up in May. I remember waiting to see or hear if he was planning anything; I didn't hear or see anything, so I decided it was my 40th and I would let no one ruin it. So, I started plans for my birthday. The first thing he announced when he saw I was making my plans was, "Yuh know sey I don't get paid until afta yuh birthday, don't it?"

I replied, "Really, you had a whole year to prepare; how come I could prepare for your birthday, but you couldn't prepare for mine?" It's funny how things can happen as there was this incident before my birthday where he said they stole his phone at work, and by the next day, he'd got a new phone. The man had an iPhone, so you know the excess isn't cheap, and he quickly found that money, but claiming at the same time he can't afford my birthday until he gets paid. How convenient for him. I remember saying to him, "I now know where your priorities lie." I'm here writing, and I still can't believe what really happened and how this man treated me.

Upon making plans, I had arranged for the party to be in a private room in a restaurant, where I could decorate the room how I liked. I asked him to pay the lady who would decorate the room, as I'd had a conversation with her, and she was happy to get paid after the party. He looked at me and said, "you know I don't get paid until after your birthday?" to which I confirmed to him she would wait until then to get paid, when I told him how much he had to pay he then said, "Who told you I was planning to give you so much?" £150 it cost to do the decorations and this man was saying this to me, me his wife, the wife that just celebrated his 40th and put the effort in it, he had a trip as well as he still had a birthday celebration before we went on holiday, which was all done and paid for by me, even with everything that he had done, he was still being an asshole.

This was the same man over the years he would only get me an anniversary gift when he saw I got him something, then he would run out and get me some Tesco flowers and a card. I would always do something special for him come Valentine's Day, our anniversary, Father's Day, etc. you name it, even randomly, sometimes I would treat him, not only on special days. The only time he made an effort for me was Christmas as he had to because it was a family moment and, obviously, he had to look good in front of everyone else.

I used to sometimes think, was it because I am HIV positive why he would treat me this way. He used to say things like; "I know you don't love me," and I would find myself trying to prove I loved him, which is why I would try to do things for him, but nothing was ever enough for him. He would happily receive the gifts. It was as if he thought he was entitled, and he would act as if this was something I was supposed to be doing for him. When on holidays in Jamaica, he would act like he loved taking care of me in front of his mom. He would say things like, "I take care of my wife, yuh nuh," which was obviously a lie. He would sometimes manipulate me and say things to my face like, "yuh know I like to take care of my wife, don't it?" and would repeat it until I would agree with him as I was in shock because I couldn't believe he was literally saying that to my face. This man did nothing for me and if he did, he would talk about it as if it was a chore or an ordeal, not something he had pleasure in doing. He would say, "yuh know mi nuh fraid to spend my money and give my wife everything." No wonder why I became so depressed. His manipulation was on another level. This was some deep shit I was dealing with.

The only other times he would make an effort was when I threatened to end the marriage and I would stop having sex with him for weeks, then he would pull his hand out of his ass and actually try. Which showed me he knew what to do but refused to do it because he was horrible. I found him to be badly insecure. Over the years, he would keep on saying that he knew I didn't love him but hopefully one day I would learn to love him. Then he would say things like, "I know you don't like me," because he would want me to prove my love to him constantly. If he said he loved me, and I didn't say it back straight away, he would vex and even probably get into a tantrum.

I used to say to him, "I don't have to say I love you too, every time you say you love me, I can say my I love you's whenever I want to. I shouldn't have to feel pressured into saying something at the same time as you say it."

Sometimes I wanted to tear my eyes open or even drag out my hair because of the stupid petty behaviour I was dealing with.

The first time I told him I was done with the marriage was at the beginning of 2020. I was dead serious, as I'd had enough by now. I couldn't carry on any longer. The pandemic hit and we were stuck with each other for the next two years. He would make the effort then, but as soon as he thought everything was ok, he went right back into tantrum mode. The thing is, this behaviour has many levels and for the next two years I was sure to meet those levels. I still didn't know what I was going through, wasn't sure what to call it. At the time, I heard the term narcissist, and I noticed it matched a lot of his behaviour and so, I would call it what it was.

But it wouldn't be until I had fallen into a deep depression, and I decided I needed a therapist, as I couldn't carry on like this. I used to ask myself, "What is it that's in me that I would attract a man like this?"

Depression sat on me like someone would sit on a chair and it refused to get up. The depression hit me terribly or should I say I recognised I was depressed at the end of 2020; I was in the process of doing a project creating and publishing an anthology book with eight authors called *Flying Without Wings*, this was my first time being a lead author of a collaborative book project. I had the responsibility of getting all eight authors to write a chapter for this book. Some of them writing for the very first time. It was exciting doing this project, but at the same time; I fell into a depression and this was while delivering tasks for the authors to do, and having to still show up and be present.

I realised I was functioning with depression; while I was working for BT and working from home, I would be going to bed and rolling out of bed and starting the computer, not even brushing my teeth or washing my face. Looking back, it's like I was a zombie.

It was easy to get away with as it was lockdown and everyone was home, so my colleagues and I would only see each other online, so no effort had to be made to look camera ready, except for my face and the top part of my body, that was easy no one would know I hadn't taken a bath and that I put on a clean top to look fresh for the camera, no one could smell my mouth and know that I hadn't brushed my teeth for a few days now and that I probably was not thinking to do it anytime soon. I could create a spot at home where the background looked good and it's safe as it's on camera and others will only see what the camera is focused on. No one had to see that I hadn't cleaned my house for God knows how long and no one could smell that something wasn't right in my house.

Part of the depression was that I would do a lot of shopping for clothes and shoes online, buying things I didn't need, by this time my stepdaughters wouldn't be visiting as it was lockdown and because of that I would be packing up the room with the things I was buying. I had zero motivation to do anything; I tried doing my art and the things I was creative at. I remember also that some of the reason I wasn't having a bath was because I didn't want to have sex with my husband anymore and that seemed easier to do, as I could say, I hadn't showered. By now I had lost all interest in my marriage, and anything intimate to do with him. I was in such a dark place I had brought myself to a place of not taking care of me at all because I wanted him to not like me anymore. I wanted him to be disgusted and leave me. But none of my depressed actions made him leave and it was as if he didn't care as he never mentioned it or asked if I was ok, as any normal husband would do. There was zero concern from him. He said absolutely nothing about me not bathing or cleaning the house. His only concern was that I wasn't giving him sex and he seemed to think I was having an affair. Wow, imagine I wasn't bathing myself; I wasn't going anywhere and because I'm not having sex with you, I'm having an affair?? With whom? When I think about it now, it is so shocking. The level of abuse I was going through, the level of breaking me he was doing, is unbelievable.

This was dark, really dark. How could I have let this happen to me? When did we get here? Can someone really break you mentally, slowly picking pieces away from you emotionally? Nothing I was telling anyone around me made sense to them. No one got what I was saying to them, as it was so surreal. I could barely make sense of what I was telling them myself. It was very petty, and he was so insecure and broken that his primary aim was to break me down to his level. And he did this on a deep psychological level.

Then one day, I was lying in bed and suddenly, the scent of my vagina hit me, and in that moment, I remembered I didn't even care and that's when the penny dropped, and I suddenly realised something was definitely wrong with me. This wasn't me; I was someone who took pride in myself and my home and now I was nowhere near doing that. I wasn't cleaning the house at all, nothing was getting done and I realised as well that I was the only one doing things in the home, because everything had stopped and the other person living with me didn't care to do it or have any concern about it either. Nothing was being said, hence the reason I probably took so long to notice my life had suddenly become a mess.

I refused to have sex with my husband at the time too, which contributed to me not bathing because I didn't want him to touch me, I think this was because of the incident that happened earlier in our marriage, with the other woman, this situation messed my head up as I couldn't understand how someone could do this especially so early in their marriage, those first few months were supposed to be our honeymoon period, we were supposed to be in love. How could anyone else be getting your attention, especially on that level?

Everything about me suddenly became messy and dirty and smelly. I didn't have a bath for days or probably weeks at a time. I noticed I had dark patches on my skin, and then I would realise it was dirt. I felt disgusted with myself but still the motivation was not there to wash my body. The bedrooms were cluttered with clothes and shoes, which I mentioned earlier was from shopping aimlessly online. These were not even things I needed. The room was full within a few months of lockdown; the rooms were full of clothes and shoes all over, the beds in the rooms were covered, if you went into the room for the first time you wouldn't think beds were in there. And this really happened since the lockdown, as his daughters would come down for the weekends before and they did have a room to themselves, to move about and do as they pleased, so what the heck happened?? I wasn't going anywhere, but still felt the need to be buying clothes and shoes. All the money I was working for, I used to buy things I didn't need or even want. I learnt later it was part of me being depressed. Everything I was going through was because of my deep depression.

Getting up to make myself a cup of tea or prepare food for myself was hard to do. I was hungry but wasn't motivated to go get food. My appetite wasn't there. I would lie in bed the whole day, especially on the days I wasn't working. I would start to book sick days as I started to not have the strength or the courage to work anymore. My motivation was completely missing. It was gone and nowhere to be found. I felt weak in my body and mind. When I got up out of the bed, it was like the dead rising, slow and sluggish. Most times, I had to talk myself into getting up and out of the bed. These were bleak moments, ones when I look back, I can't believe I was even there. It now feels like it was a dream because how real can it be to go to that place and really survive from it?

A light hit me, and I realised this was a big messy situation. My head, my house, my body, my everything was a mess, a big humiliating MESS! What a thing, what has really happened Yanique?

I had to get help. I must get help, and that's exactly what I did. I remember phoning a friend of mine and asking for the number of a therapist and explained to her exactly what had been happening to me. She gave me the number and I made contact to confirm how to get started. This was the scariest thing I had to do. I think I was shaking on the phone while talking to a therapist and booking my date to start.

ELEVEN

ELEVEN

My first therapy session was scary. I almost cancelled as I was so afraid of the unknown. Being from my cultural background, this was never an option or something you would resort to, as if it reached that level, it simply means you are mad or crazy. That's what they called my Dad. I was someone who grew up thinking my Dad was a madman and following everyone else and labelling him worthless. He had a mental illness, and I didn't know, as we knew nothing about what that meant. It wasn't even a word I ever heard of my whole life living in Jamaica. The word for that was either crazy or mad. I now can imagine how my Dad must have felt all his life. I cry sometimes, thinking about it, as I now felt sorry for him. He died not knowing he was loved, especially by his only child, how horrible that must have felt. I can imagine how those things would probably have caused him to get worse with his illness when he couldn't get the love and understanding from his only child. I remember when I heard of my Dad's passing; I was crying almost most of the day and couldn't understand how I was tearing up like this for a man I didn't even know. But I realised it was tears of regret and guilt. I felt ashamed that I never took the time to get to know him and actually get to understand his illness; I didn't even know what his mental illness was. That's how far from reality I was when it came to this condition of being mentally ill.

Taking this leap to have therapy showed how bad things had become and I had to make a decision for me or else it would probably be a different story being told now, probably a story being told by someone else. The most I heard about mental health or depression was when I started living in the UK. Hearing about it was one thing, but understanding it was on a whole different level, as most times this thing called depression isn't understood until you have experienced it. And let me say this: I experienced it. I experienced it on a whole deeper level. Depression suddenly became a part of my life.

I had what you call psychodynamic therapy. My therapist asked me to tell her about my childhood, thinking I had the perfect childhood I started, but to my surprise I suddenly realised it wasn't as perfect as I thought it was. There was a lot that was coming up that I didn't even know was there. I was solving my own issues; I was identifying with my emotions and picking up where these emotions would have started from; I was recognising why I would behave a certain way; I realised why I was so angry most of the time and quick to argue and prove I was right, no matter what.

I talked about growing up with my grandmother and my aunty and explaining what life was like. And suddenly, a memory I had forgotten came out of nowhere. I suddenly remembered that my grandmother used to come home from work in the evenings and would question and ask me if I had been beaten today and would search me for the scars. I remember feeling scared and then would hear my grandmother arguing with my aunty saying things like, "Mi nuh tell yuh sey yuh nuh fi put yuh hands on har?" my grandmother would be so upset, but this was something that kept happening until my grandmother had no choice but to bring me to work with her. This was a memory that suddenly appeared in my first session, and it suddenly dawned on me why my grandmother would take me everywhere she went. My aunty was my abuser, and she has been my abuser all my life. Things were making sense clearly now. Memories of how my aunty was the bully in the family. I experienced her bullying my mom all her life and trying to turn me against my mother by manipulating me. She would say nasty things about my mother. If my mother would discipline me, she would turn it around and manipulate the situation to make me think my mother was the worst. The scales were dropping from my eyes. I had experienced so much toxicity with my aunty throughout my life and didn't even realise what this thing was until now. Telling the things and the journey I had been on with this woman in my life is a whole chapter, which, as you read on, all will be revealed.

This session was incredible. I was the one talking and solving my own issues. I loved every moment of my therapy session and decided I would complete the six weeks of therapy sessions and get on my journey of healing. During my sessions, I spoke about my marriage and what I was experiencing at the time, and my therapist confirmed my husband was a narcissist, but he was one on a psychological level, and this was dangerous, and in most cases, they would never change.

She helped me to recognise what I was going through, and I started to see it more in him and was able to call him out each time he played one of his mind games.

By the new year 2021, I started my second therapy session and would carry on every other week until my six sessions were finished. But while doing my therapy, I would create coping mechanisms daily, and one of those would be my early morning routine. I would get up at 5 am every morning at first. I started at 30 days and ended up continuing until I had a few ladies who joined me a few of the months. We met on Zoom every morning at 6:00 am and would finish at 7:00 am. I would do my session from 5:00 am and then join the ladies from 6:00 am. I had to get drastic with my healing, so this journey was so important to me because I wanted to make changes and I learnt some time ago that for things to change, you yourself must change. And so, I changed the little things we all tend to take for granted. We don't realise how much a little a day of doing these things can be so powerful. I prayed, meditated, did my affirmations, reading, journaling and exercise, this was done for one hour, 10 minutes of this, 20 minutes of that, all split to add up to one hour. I was amazed at how many books I had read within a month, how much stuff I had journaled about, how my mind was making me feel and my body felt amazing, too.

Prior to starting my morning routine, I had stopped eating meat and was doing a lot of detoxing and intermittent fasting; I was losing weight and regaining my confidence. I went for walks and did my exercise indoors when I couldn't go out to walk. I was smiling inside and out. My mind, my body, and my emotions felt healthy. I felt good all over. This was the best start to my day as I would be on fire, ready to do the day and achieve what I needed for me. I became aware of my emotions and how I was feeling in the moment and by being aware; I could make the changes I needed to make for me to feel how I know I wanted to feel for that day.

I wasn't interested in my marriage. I would still try but I wasn't 100% in. I was done by now; I was tired of it and wanted out. I think my husband knew but wouldn't say anything but would taunt me every day, telling me I had someone else, he would always accuse me of cheating, he would go as far as to say he's had evidence and that I should own up to it and tell him the truth. This accusation went on throughout being married to this man for five years. Until the day he was leaving, he was still accusing me of cheating and having someone else.

He tried doing things, like throwing a party for my birthday, booking for us to go away for our honeymoon and celebrating Christmas that year was totally different to what we usually do. We went away that Christmas and visited family. By then it was way too late because there was so much damage with no apology or reassurance or even recognition that he was the way he was. Everything was getting brushed under the carpet by him, nothing being resolved and that for me was keeping us in a cycle, as we would always end up in the same place arguing about the same things and no change being made on his part. He was trying to be a better husband he would say, but refused to let us try to be friends too. Once he looked at me with scorn and said, "We will never be friends," there was no closeness. He would only touch me when he wanted sex. That's the only time he tried to be intimate. Otherwise, he wouldn't cuddle, touch, or do anything like that. And when I mentioned it, he would get upset and play the victim and not speak to me because I had upset him. This used to happen a lot, too. He loved playing the victim. Like the time I found out about his WhatsApp affair, I called all our family members and told everyone about what he did. He then turned around upset with me for telling everyone and played the victim and didn't speak to me for a while. He got upset because I was upset about something he'd done to hurt my feelings and damage our marriage. He acted as if he wanted me to apologise for telling on him. He would try to turn the whole situation and make it about him and how he was feeling, and disregarded what he'd done to cause the situation in the first place.

By the end of Christmas 2021, I was ready for a change, and that's exactly what happened in the new year. I told him on his birthday January 4th he had to leave now and that this time this was it, no more trying as it had been five years, and we were still not moving forward, and I needed to be by myself now. I needed my me time now and I couldn't have that with him being around. Especially with him not being interested in working on himself, as he didn't feel like there was anything wrong with him and his behaviours. I am not saying I was innocent during the marriage. We all have our faults, but I faced up to them and decided to work on my marriage and myself. But it takes two to do the journey, and if I'm going to be doing it alone while I'm married to someone who is causing more damage, then it made sense for me to be alone and continue to work on me all by myself, in a stress-free environment.

Because of his pride, he left in January and took his things with him. He tried not to leave, but I wouldn't allow it and I had to clarify that he had to GO! He got the picture after a while and, as I said, his pride worked in my favour, and he left.

How did I feel?

I felt a sense of relief, like a weight had been lifted off me. The house even felt much lighter and felt like I had cleared something negative out of the house. This feeling was amazing. I was alone and anyone that knows me knows I love my alone time. It's very golden to me and I treasure the moments when I am all alone. Some days, it felt surreal. I couldn't believe he was gone. I wasn't missing him or thinking about taking him back. I felt good; I was in a great headspace plus I had things and people around who helped to motivate me and made me feel happier.

At one point he started texting me and became nasty, then he would be nice one day and then nasty the next. So, I had to block him, then when he realised, he was blocked on my mobile phone he started to send emails.

I could go on and on about all the things that happened but that would take a whole book by itself. I shared a few of the things I am less shameful about, some things I know I have pushed aside so as not to remember them. Honestly, my second marriage was the most terrible experience I've had with someone of the opposite sex, and I'm not saying this out of anger. It's the truth. His behaviour caused me to go places I never knew I could have gone, said things and done things I didn't even know I had in me. At one point, I felt like I was the abuser because I was defending myself and the level of how I had to be defending myself left me feeling like the abuser. He brought out the worst in me. What's the point of being with someone who brings out the worst in me when I have so much goodness, purity, love, kindness, and life to offer?

I had a conversation once with someone who assumed I needed to have a relationship with Jesus, as this wouldn't be happening to me. I had to let them know that it's because of my relationship with Jesus I am still here and could go through and come through. Some people will question you when they don't understand and make assumptions, too. When they have never experienced what you've been through, they will come with all sorts. I remember asking, "If I was telling you that this man was beating me every day, would you still be advising me to stay and question my relationship with God?" to which they answered no. So, I said, "Well, he might as well have been beating me because that's exactly what it felt like." and then I guess everyone would understand what I was really going through and appreciate the decision I have made to end my marriage.

Earlier, I started to share about a family member and said I would need a whole chapter for that one. Well, here we go.

When I was deported back to Jamaica. I entrusted my kids to a family member who was living with me and my first husband. At the time, we weren't married yet. This person was an older aunty for me. Actually, she was my mom's sister.

I had sent for her when I was pregnant with my second daughter. What happened if you're following the story, was that my older daughter was sent to Jamaica to visit the family and she would spend most of the time with my aunty, as she wasn't working. Since my mom had a job and couldn't commit to watching my daughter, we decided she would spend most of her time with my aunt. There were times my aunty would make it seem as if my mom wasn't interested in keeping my daughter. But as time went on, I would understand that wasn't the case.

My aunt's constant negative comments about my mom created a rift between us over the years, leading me to develop resentment towards my mother. My aunty had a style where, if my mom disciplined me, she my aunty would exaggerate it and literally pull the wool over my eyes, and obviously being a child, I was easily manipulated by her and the things they would say about my mom. Her influence against my mom persisted until I reached adulthood.

I would always, over the years say things like this was my favourite aunty. We were close, as she would make sure she built that relationship between us. She was evil, but it took years of abuse and manipulation before the scales would fall off my eyes and ears.

When it was time for my daughter to return to the UK, I asked my mother if she would like to come with her, as being pregnant again, I would need the help to prepare for my second child. However, my mom, who is always the caring sister, thought it would be better to send for my aunt instead since she wasn't working and needed the break more than my mom did. So, my mom was kind enough to let her take her place. Little did we know this would be the biggest mistake of my life.

My daughter returned to the UK with my aunty in September 2002, two months after my second daughter was born. This was a feeling that I can't explain, as I missed my daughter so much and was so happy that she was back home. She left the UK when she was only 10 months and returned when she was 2yrs old. She spent a year and two months. So, you can imagine my joy. If you're a mom, I'm sure you know exactly where I'm coming from.

We all quickly settled back in and started life. Britanie started infant school and because my aunty was here to help as I would have work, at the time I worked in the nail salon on the corner of Soho Rd and Rookery Rd in Handsworth, Birmingham. I was working six days a week and would need the help with the kids. My aunty would take Britanie to school and would help look after Chinia. She would do most of the school run if their dad was busy with work, too. It was a perfect setup as I didn't have to send them to nursery and would pay that money to my aunty; she was good with the girls and took great care of them. She would teach them things from an early age and so after a while, they were really advanced for their ages. Don't get me wrong, they were naturally bright girls, but my aunty would go the extra mile with them, which I'm thankful that she did.

This set up would go on for some time. This made it easy for me to work and not worry about the girls and they were in great hands. At least that's what I thought. Don't get me wrong, she never abused them, but remember I mentioned she was a manipulator, and she manipulated me against my mom, well years to come I would realise all along she was doing the same exact thing with my daughters against me. The evil this woman brought with her from Jamaica was on a whole new level.

As the girls got older, they were around four and two when the big deportation happened. I had travelled on false documents and on my way back from a short trip; I was held at the airport and was questioned about the passport I was travelling on. I had to come clean and own up to what had happened. This was the beginning of the greatest disastrous years of my life pertaining to my aunt.

This woman lived with me; she saw most of the abuse I went through with the girls' dad before I got deported back to Jamaica. So, while in Jamaica, I would let her know everything I'm doing or did. Not knowing she was telling the girls' dad, bringing back information to him about me. This was happening for some time, but I didn't even realise. I noticed whenever I would tell her about an argument I had with him, she would mostly be on his side, but I still didn't think it's because she had suddenly sided with him. There was a time we had some argument about him taking my name off the land title, this was a piece of land we bought in Jamaica it was a big blowup between us and my aunt heard about the argument and phoned me cussing, saying, "Why are you trying to hold on to the man's things, it's not your land so take your name off it." It's not my land?? We lived together. This was between me and him, so why was she suddenly getting involved in my arguments with this man? And why as my aunty would you be on his side and not trying to at least give me some good advice, no you're angry with me and cussing me too. This was so weird because I couldn't believe what I was hearing. Then I picked up that I couldn't trust her anymore, that something was off. I couldn't quite put my finger to it, but something was definitely off.

I thought to myself now, at the time when she started to behave funny, it was coming near for me to come back home. Could it be that she didn't want me to come back home? It sounded as if she was getting comfy playing the role of Yanique's life. She would tell him of things that would happen, or I would do, because I noticed he would ask certain questions out of the blue or make certain statements and I knew someone was talking off their mouth. But why? Why was this happening? What would cause my own aunty to suddenly turn on me like this? Why would she side with this man?

She knew I wanted to leave him and would say things like, so what you going to do? How would you manage? She wasn't happy about me leaving, obviously, as she and her sons were benefitting off him too, so it was clear that me wanting to leave would interrupt any extra payments she was getting, especially payments that were done behind my back.

By the time I was back in the UK. Things got worse. I felt like I was living in someone else's house, the home I once knew wasn't home to me anymore. My aunty had a certain authority suddenly and it was like she was the woman of the house now. She would watch everything I did. Being on the house phone became a problem. I would hear from time to time, the both of them (her and the kids' dad) whispering about me. She would make certain remarks about me. It was very clear that I was the stranger in the house. I would go to sleep every night crying and praying to God, asking for a way out. I had suicidal thoughts, but I would remember the girls and instead broke down crying until I fell asleep. The tension of this betrayal was deep.

Things were getting so bad and intense. One night as me and the kids' dad were having one of our arguments, he blurted out something and asked me a question about something I did when I was in Jamaica. Before I could reply, there was my aunty bursting out of her room and giving him the answer and right in front of my face she started to tell him of everything that I did in Jamaica, things he wasn't supposed to know, even things he didn't even need to know. Oh yes, she ripped everything out and spewed it all over the floor. I stood there in shock, because some things she was telling were also lies she made up. *Wow*, I thought, standing there looking at her spilling the beans, *you hate me this much*? I couldn't in a million years believe what I was witnessing. She went to town with me that night. Not only that, but when he left, she broke down and started to bawl saying, "Look what you made me do!!!" ME MADE YOU DO??? SHOCKER!

Until this day, I don't get the bitterness I was experiencing from this woman. Where was this jealousy and hatred coming from and why??

After everything that was happening, I couldn't take it anymore and one day we ended up in a physical fight. I called the police and got them to tell her to leave. As she had her flat, and made it clear to me on numerous occasions that she wasn't leaving, when I said to her, "Why don't you leave and go to your flat?" She blatantly refused. So, this day was my moment, and I told the police everything and told them she had her flat and they made her leave that day.

Over the next few days, she would pop by and collect her things bit by bit, slowly but surely, until she didn't have any need to be visiting. This would be the beginning of us not talking for quite a few years, as I wanted nothing to do with her.

The girls would still go to visit her, even when me and their dad did finally separate.

I knew I should have not let her be so involved in the girls' lives after everything that happened. I don't know why I could have allowed her to be so involved; it was like she felt entitled to be in the girls' lives. I am grateful that she has been there for them, but she was too involved and now I'm here writing my book with regrets about her and the relationship she has with my daughters.

There are so many things that I could go through and talk about this toxic and horrible relationship with my aunty. It's heavy and I wish I truly had the energy to think of more things to write. What I've written so far is what I could bear to remember and write about. I pray daily about learning how to forgive her and let go of the anger and the things she has done to me over the years of my life. I get angry with myself at times as I blame myself for allowing her to get all this involvement in me and my daughter's lives. How could I have allowed her to manipulate and lie and get away with so much?

These days we do not have a relationship, because that is best for me and my mental health moving forward. There are even things she has done lately, with the same bitterness towards me, trying to get involved in me and my daughters' lives, calling my pastor and bishop and telling them my business, things about my life, the life she is no longer involved in. I shake my head now and all I can ask is WHY?

I told God I'm leaving this one in His hands and praying that I learn to forgive her and get rid of this anger for her, as she's not worth it. It's heavy and I know this healing journey is a process and it's about allowing myself to process the healing. There is some deepness to dig through, but I know with prayer this too shall pass.

TWELVE

TWELVE

This is my story, this is my song- My name is Yanique Taylor & I am living with HIV!

I never ever would have dreamed that this was something that would happen to me. I would be very careful and safe when it came to sex. So how could this have happened to me? Anyway, it did, and I have now come to terms with the fact that this is something that can happen to anyone, anyone having sex, that is. This was someone I trusted (the person I caught HIV from) and felt very disappointed at first and still do instead of angry. It shows that you can't trust anyone, because even if you're married you can still get it, because the only person you can trust is yourself, as you know exactly what's going on especially when you take responsibility to know your status and protect yourself. Someone can say trust them, but are they saying it knowing their status, or because they don't look or feel unwell? Because you would be surprised at the amount of people that are ignorant towards knowing anything about HIV. Some people think it's only within the LGBT community, or if you're on drugs or if you contract it from a blood transfusion; not realising that it can happen to anyone having sex too, heterosexual or homosexual anyone can get it.

After hearing about my diagnosis. I had to start on medication immediately. When I first started taking the medication, it was two tablets every day. I had to take them at the same time every day; now I am down to taking one tablet a day. So, I have to set an alarm to remind myself daily. This is hard, as it is something new. In the first year, after my diagnosis, I had clinical depression and didn't realise it. I suddenly started to feel low, and sleep wasn't my best friend anymore. At first, I didn't realise that these things were caused by the tablets. I wasn't aware of the side effects; I wasn't really paying attention as I think by then I was moving with the motions and doing what I was told. I have to do my blood test every three to four months, which is a horrible feeling and situation for me. They take about seven bottles of blood off me; the needle is painful and so uncomfortable, especially at first. I have to do a urine test too, check my weight and take my blood pressure. The great thing about this whole situation now is that I know my status and my health. I am now on the priority list. As soon as anything comes up about my health, I am a priority patient so must be seen as soon as possible.

For the first two years every time I visited the clinic, shame took over and I would cry immensely as the was now my forever reality. Don't get me wrong, the doctors and nurses at the clinic made me feel at ease and there was never any judgement from them. Which, after a while, made it easier to go and do my regular check-ups. After a while I did start to look forward to going, as now my viral level was going down and I am now undetectable and that means I cannot transmit the virus as long as I'm on my medication, which I have to take every day.

Don't get me wrong, the nurse told me that I can continue my normal everyday life without being a risk to other people, and that it changes nothing, because it's transmitted sexually, through using shared needles and mother to baby transmission. I can't affect anyone by touching, sharing food or hugging. Normal everyday activities would not affect anyone. So, I could go back to work as usual without being worried about anyone being affected.

People often say "you look so healthy" which is due to being on my medication. So, I look healthy, but mentally and emotionally it's taken a toll on me. My new reality with HIV looks like some days are great, some are good and then there are the bad and worst days. Those bad and worst days want to be my most days, and sometimes they are, but God has truly been with me through all these bad and worst days. I refuse to believe that God has brought me this far to leave me. So, I will continue to trust in Him always. I will continue to seek His guidance and His will for my life on this continued journey.

After a few months, my HIV status became U=U.

U=U means that people with HIV who achieve and maintain an undetectable viral load—the amount of HIV in the blood—by taking antiretroviral therapy (ART) daily as prescribed cannot sexually transmit the virus to others. Thus, treatment for HIV is a powerful arrow in the quiver of HIV prevention tools.

The shame I was feeling was on another level, as where I am from this was a big stigma and people would class you as dirty and nasty. But as time went by and I learned more about the disease, I became less and less shameful. I looked at the positive side of things now. There is so much still for me to learn, and I am slowly learning. These days I am now on one tablet a day. My side effects are huge, and I'm learning to manage and deal with them on a daily basis.

My Medical conditions:

1. Extreme Lethargy
2. Endogenous Depression
3. Chronic Insomnia
4. Anaemia
5. Headache
6. Memory loss
7. Forgetfulness
8. Heavy Periods
9. Fibroid uterus
10. Adenomyosis
11. High Cholesterol
12. Joint pain
13. Raised Rh Factor

Although my HIV viral load is fully suppressed and CD4 lymphocytes count is above 500 cells/mm3, I remain markedly disabled because of existing co-morbidities.

The reason I've decided to share my story now is to bring healing and awareness, to break the shame and stigma around HIV/AIDS. To educate people and let them know how important it is to get tested and know your status, especially within the black Christian community. Knowing your status keeps you safe and keeps others safe, too. People need to understand that none of us is exempt from it, especially when having sex. You can catch it in other ways too: Most people who get HIV get it through anal or vaginal sex, or sharing needles, syringes, or other drug injection equipment (for example, cookers).

There is so much to learn and know. Just do your research, ask your doctor. They are more than happy to supply you with the information you need. But most of all, get tested and know your status. You really owe this to yourself and others. The more of us doing this, the more we are making our communities safer and healthier.

My True reality with DEPRESSION

I had been separated from my marriage now for about a year; I was on my healing journey, writing my book and feeling good about finally wanting to tell my story. I was also in a place where I stopped talking with my family and took myself away from them as I now realise it was too toxic for me. I had a lot of unforgiveness for my mother and my family and people I felt who had done me wrong, which I didn't really understand, had a big impact on me tremendously.

Throughout my life, I had to deal with a lot of rejection upon rejection. Which I suddenly realised started from my mother and my dad not being active in my life and I realised this from me starting to write my book. Writing this book is a part of my healing journey, and bwoy oh bwoy, what a journey that has been.

During the process of writing this book, my triggers were getting closer and closer. I would be very emotional this minute and the next minute I'm fine. You would have spoken to me on the phone or seen me in the flesh and I would look and sound happy, motivated and ready to take on the world and within an hour after I'm on the floor at home screaming and bawling, being angry with either myself or someone. I would make irrational decisions, like spending money on takeaways, which was a lot because I was anxious about going into the shops and would have to talk myself into getting the takeaway.

I noticed a few things happening to me and suddenly I realised I was depressed; I didn't want to answer my phone to anyone, I wouldn't reply to text messages or WhatsApp, I would become too overwhelmed, my curtains not opened for days, my room was in constant darkness, I was in bed the whole day if I didn't have anywhere to go, forgetting to eat, not bathing or brushing my teeth, as long as I was home I would be in the bed sleeping, bawling. Feelings of shame, feelings of rejection were upon me. I didn't go on social media as it made me feel overwhelmed as everyone else's lives seemed so put together. I had zero motivation to do the things I love, like journaling, cooking, bathing and taking care of myself, my art, blogging, everything I loved doing was gone from me. I couldn't find the urge to even piss or shit. I would lie in bed for hours, struggling to get up and go piss. The worst thing was, all this was going on and I would go out with a smile on my face, all washed up for that day, smelling and looking good, but inside me was dark and lonely with not even a candle to burn and shed some light. I was doing badly but couldn't say anything. How can I say these things? This is embarrassing. Who would or could I tell? Nobody! I thought I am going to die with this one, because no one will understand. I couldn't show up looking depressed. I didn't know how to look bad in public.

Plus, I was grieving for my friend and colleague who died suddenly on September 3rd 2022. I would have panic attacks about not waking up when I go to sleep, fear of dying. Insomnia kicked in, in the worst way possible. Don't get me wrong, I was struggling with some insomnia because of my medication, but when the sudden death of Chantel happened, the insomnia got worse. I wasn't sleeping at all. I would be up the whole day and the whole night. If I got some sleep, it would be for about 2-3 hours at a time. No wonder the depression got worse. There was so much going on in my life at the time or for that year, I should say. 2022 What a year in review. I look back now and can't explain how I made it through those months. I can only say God brought me through.

You see, depression will never be really understood unless you have been in it? I don't think you can hear about it and understand. No way, I believe you can only get it when you have experienced it at some level. In my opinion, you will never understand depression until you have lived it.

It's a language that only those who feel it know.

"Tell me about your depression, Yan," a question asked one day. I thought about it for a few seconds and then out of nowhere I started to off load everything about what I was truly going through. I felt like I was a child again and I was crying and crying and crying. It felt like my floodgate was burst open and everything I was going through came right out. No filter, plain hardcore truth pouring out of me. I cried for three days straight non-stop. My eyes were swollen and red. I was broken down; I was suddenly at this place where I couldn't carry this load anymore. I had to drop the bags and run for help!

I even had to be real with my therapist once and for all. She got my GP to phone me and book me in for an appointment. They started me on Sertraline, an antidepressant. Wow Yan. You really doing this? I asked myself. Yes, I answered myself. It's about time you think about you and what's good for you now. Don't be bothered by what anyone thinks. You know what you are going through, and the only way God is going to help is if you do what you are supposed to do for you. Was this a part of my healing? Yes, it was. I couldn't have gone through so much in life and not come to this place. I only wish it had happened sooner. But this is what happens when you decide to tell your story with truth, naked and raw.

I now have regular therapy sessions. When I first started on the Sertraline tablets, it was horrible. They started me off on 50mg and nothing was happening, and I wasn't sleeping. Then they put it up to 100mg and I still couldn't sleep. This is the struggle I'm going through at the time of writing this book. It's March 13th 2023. This is my reality currently. I hope within the next few months I can have a different story about my continued healing journey.

THIRTEEN

THIRTEEN

I don't know much about my father, apart from the little I've heard about him over my life span. I am hoping to one day to find out more about my Dad and probably even write a book about him. I bet he had an interesting life. One thing I knew about him was he had mental health issues. Not sure what those issues were, as growing up, I used to just follow everyone else ignorantly and accuse him of being worthless. *"How yuh can have one pickney and don't care about her?"* those were my thoughts then. I used to be so angry and confused with him. I was his only child. Yes, I am an only child for both parents. Imagine that. Your only child and you don't care. But I didn't recognise that he was ill and that was something out of his control. I now wish I had more knowledge on the topic of mental health and really understood about it. But I didn't. I wish I got to know him more for myself.

I used to see him walking up and down the road most days, where my grandparents lived and he lived too. He always had a cutlass with him and would be dressed in khaki suit, uniform outfit, with his back pockets filled with papers. I would sometimes see him sitting on someone's roof top, there looking around and he would wave at me and smile. One thing for sure he never left his cutlass.

There is this story I've heard about him and his mental state. He has a sister who lived with him in their parents' home, I think this was after their parents died. He never really liked the idea of with my aunty living with him, as for him it was his dad house as they had different dads, so in his head she shouldn't be living in the house too.

So, his plan to run them out of the house was to poo in a bucket and then leave it in his bedroom and lock the door of his room so no one could get in, then he left and went bush to spend a few days not sure how long it was, but it was long enough for the house to start stinking. By now everyone living in the house was getting worried and frustrated because they couldn't tell where this smell was coming from. When they finally realised where it was coming from, they had to kick the door down to get in the room. Let's just say it wasn't a very good experience for them. That's one of the stories I would hear.

At times now wish I had more knowledge on the topic of mental health and really understood about it. But I didn't. I wish I got to know my Dad more. A very attractive man, small, and petite with a nice dark complexion. He had so much hair on his head at one point I thought he had locs. But I realised he would get his hair groomed when he could and would tie it up in a turban style.

It's strange because there are times when I miss my Dad, and I think how can you miss someone you never knew? He died in January 2012. I remember when I heard the news of his death; I cried as if I knew this man and I was so broken-hearted. I was planning that same year to go to Jamaica and the plan was to go look for him and spend some time talking. This was never to be because he died only a few months before I travelled back home.

R.I.P. Dad. Hopefully, one day I can really get to know more about you. ***Baldwin Constantine Taylor, August 19th 1956 – January 17th 2012.***

Mummy

As I have gotten older, and especially since I have actually talked with someone about how I am truly feeling, I have come to the realisation that my Mom does really love me at least the best way she knows how to. She might not have done it verbally, but I can see now that she showed it in her actions. Whenever I go to Jamaica as an adult, my Mom will wash for me, even my underwear. She will do the little things that she knows best to do. I appreciate it because people can only deliver what they know how to deliver. Her way of delivering her love to me is by doing. Maybe one day we can reach that place of hugging each other, laughing and crying together. Loving on each other as the mother and daughter we are. Meaning it doesn't have to look like what society portrays as long as we are both happy and comfortable with how we choose to show our affection to each other.

I too love my mother. And I know there are things about me she would love to experience and would long for from her daughter. I pray we can do this; I feel good about our future together if it's the will of God.

Oh, this I have to say. I am so proud of my Mom; she passed her driving test at 63 and received her driving license. It was a moment for me as much as it was for her. I hope she realised how awesome and inspiring it is. I feel good all over for her. Next step is her car. I can't wait for the day I go back home and it's my Mom picking me up from the airport. How awesome will that be? VERY!

Overall, I have had a good life, full of experiences and no regrets. I try not to regret anything, but look at it as a learning experience. I am not the girl I used to be. The things I have done in the past, it's in the past and those are the experiences that have made me the phenomenal woman I am today. I bounced back from all that was meant to destroy me; I know I am a child of God and not to be messed with.

I am grateful always for the journey and pray that God will always give me strength to continue to go through this life of mine.

Few Lessons Learnt:

Regret nothing, learn from it, heal from it, and move on.

Be strong enough to walk away from what's hurting you, be patient enough to wait for the blessings you deserve.

Never reply when you are angry, never make a promise when you're happy, and never make a decision when you're sad.

Always know that your current situation is not your final destination. The best is yet to come.

Here are five things you should speak to yourself every day:

1. God is with me
2. I am the best
3. I can do it
4. I am a winner
5. Today is my day

Jeremiah 29:11: *"For I know the plans I have for you,' declares the LORD, 'plans to prosper you and not to harm you, plans to give you hope and a future."*

Meet Yanique

A best-selling Author, Upcoming Speaker, radio presenter and creative. She is an exciting, fun loving and proud mother of two adult daughters, a Warrior, a Survivor, a woman living with HIV. Yanique is known for her flair in the fashion world and beauty industries for over twenty years. She has run makeup workshops, vision board workshops, art therapy workshops and morning challenges with various women over the years. Her workshops are something she still runs, morning challenges on Zoom and art therapy workshops in person.

She is now also dedicating her life to sharing her naked truth, your naked truth and our naked truth through raising awareness around HIV, Depression, and Domestic Abuse. Helping others to heal as she now understands that this journey is not only about her and God will turn it around for good, what the enemy meant for evil.

GLOSSARY

(JAMAICANISMS)

Afta – After
Bawling – Crying
Bl@@%& - Swear word
Bwoy – Boy
Chile – Child
Cussing – Telling someone off
Dash wey – Throw away
Dem – Them
Dis – This
Faass – Nosey
Fi – To
Fraid – Afraid
Gonna – Going
Gyal – Girl
Har – Her
Hengland – England
Inna – Into
Jooks – Poking
Kinda – Kind of
Likkle – Little
Lick – A slap or hiding
Mek - Make
Mi – Me
Mussi – Must be
Nuff - Plenty
Nuh – Don't say

Nutten – Nothing
Pickney – Child
Pissentail - Being Cheeky
Sey - Say
Sis – Sister
Tink – Think
Weh – Where
Waan – Want
Weh yuh a go? – Where are you going?
"Yuh pretty eeen?" – You're so pretty, aren't you?
Yuh – You

Appendices

Appendix 1.

10 Things to Know About HIV Suppression

Development of antiretroviral drugs to treat HIV has turned what was once an almost always fatal infection into a manageable chronic condition. Daily antiretroviral therapy can reduce the amount of HIV in the blood to levels that are undetectable with standard tests. Staying on treatment is crucial to keep the virus suppressed. NIAID-supported research has demonstrated that achieving and maintaining a "durably undetectable" viral load (the amount of HIV in the blood) not only preserves the health of the person living with HIV but also prevents sexual transmission of the virus to an HIV-negative partner.

What is viral suppression?

Antiretroviral therapy keeps HIV from making copies of itself. When a person living with HIV begins an antiretroviral treatment regimen, their viral load drops. For almost everyone who starts taking their HIV medication daily as prescribed, viral load will drop to an undetectable level in six months or less. Continuing to take HIV medications as directed is imperative to stay undetectable.

What does it mean to be durably undetectable?

Taking antiretroviral therapy daily as prescribed to suppress HIV levels leads to an "undetectable" status. A person is considered to have a "durably undetectable" viral load if their viral load remains undetectable for at least six months after their first undetectable test result. It is essential to continue to take every pill every day as directed to maintain an undetectable viral load.

Does being durably undetectable mean that the virus has left my body?

Even when viral load is undetectable, HIV is still present in the body. The virus lies dormant inside a small number of cells in the body, called viral reservoirs. When therapy is halted by missing doses, taking a treatment holiday, or stopping treatment, the virus emerges and begins to multiply, becoming detectable in the blood again. This newly reproducing virus is infectious. It is essential to take every pill every day as directed to achieve and maintain a durably undetectable status.

How does being durably undetectable affect my risk of transmitting HIV to a sexual partner?

People living with HIV who take antiretroviral medications daily as prescribed and who achieve and then maintain an undetectable viral load have effectively no risk of sexually transmitting the virus to an HIV-negative partner.

Three large multinational research studies involving couples in which one partner was living with HIV and the other was not—HPTN 052, PARTNER and Opposites Attract—observed no HIV transmission to the HIV-negative partner while the partner with HIV had a durably undetectable viral load. These studies followed approximately 3,000 male-female and male-male couples over many years while they did not use condoms. Over the course of the PARTNER and Opposites Attract studies, couples reported engaging in more than 74,000 condomless episodes of vaginal or anal intercourse.

After I begin HIV treatment, how long does it take for the risk of sexually transmitting HIV to become effectively zero?

There is effectively no risk of sexual transmission of HIV when the partner living with HIV has achieved an undetectable viral load and then maintained it for at least six months. Most people living with HIV who start taking antiretroviral therapy daily as prescribed achieve an undetectable viral load within one to six months after beginning treatment.

A person's viral load is considered "durably undetectable" when all viral load test results are undetectable for at least six months after their first undetectable test result. This means that most people will need to be on treatment for 7 to 12 months to have a durably undetectable viral load. It is essential to take every pill every day to maintain durably undetectable status.

What happens if I stop taking antiretroviral therapy?

When therapy is stopped, viral load rebounds, and the risk of transmitting HIV to a sexual partner in the absence of other prevention methods returns. NIAID-supported research has provided clear-cut scientific evidence to support the benefits of staying on continuous antiretroviral treatment. In 2006, NIAID's large clinical trial called SMART showed that people receiving intermittent antiretroviral treatment had twice the rate of disease progression compared to those receiving continuous treatment.

Taking antiretroviral treatment daily as directed to achieve and maintain durably undetectable status stops HIV infection from progressing, helping people living with HIV stay healthy and live longer, while offering the benefit of preventing sexual transmission. Stopping and re-starting treatment can cause drug resistance to develop, making that treatment regimen ineffective and limiting future treatment options.

How often do I need to be tested to confirm that I'm durably undetectable?

According to U.S. HIV treatment guidelines, viral load typically should be measured every three to four months. People living with HIV should talk with their health care teams to determine an appropriate schedule for viral load testing.

What are viral load "blips"?

Even if a person is durably undetectable and taking antiretroviral therapy daily as prescribed, they may experience small, transient increases in viral load called "blips" followed by a decrease back to undetectable levels. Having a blip is relatively common and does not indicate that antiretroviral therapy has failed to control the virus. Scientists are working to better understand what causes blips.

How do I talk to my partner about their risk of acquiring HIV?

People living with HIV can involve their partners in their treatment plans. Research shows that adhering to treatment often can improve with support from loving relationships and from the community.

Pre-exposure prophylaxis (PrEP), in which an HIV-negative person takes antiretroviral medication to prevent infection, can be part of the conversation.

Do I still need to worry about other sexually transmitted infections?

Neither HIV treatment nor PrEP prevents other sexually transmitted infections, or STIs.

Ways to reduce the risk of STIs include having both partners tested, limiting the number of sexual partners and using condoms. Vaccines are available to prevent some STIs, including hepatitis B and human papillomavirus (HPV).

Content last reviewed on June 12, 2020

Credit: NIAID

Appendix 2.
Below is an article I found which explains a bit more about depression, especially in women:

Depression In Women: Things you should know

Being sad is a normal reaction to difficult times in life. But usually, the sadness goes away with a little time. Depression is different—it is a mood disorder that may cause severe symptoms that can affect how you feel, think, and handle daily activities such as sleeping, eating, or working. Depression is more common among women than men, likely due to certain biological, hormonal, and social factors that are unique to women.

Depression is a real medical condition.

Depression is a common but serious mood disorder. Depression symptoms can interfere with your ability to work, sleep, study, eat, and enjoy your life. Although researchers are still studying the causes of depression, current research suggests that depression is caused by a combination of genetic, biological, environmental, and psychological factors. Feeling better typically requires treatment for most individuals with depression.

You can't just 'snap out' of depression.

Well-meaning friends or family members may try to tell someone with depression to "snap out of it," " be positive," or "you can be happier if you try harder." But depression is not a sign of a person's weakness or a character flaw. The truth is that most people who experience depression need treatment to get better.

If you are a friend or family member of a woman with depression, you can offer emotional support, understanding, patience, and encouragement. But never dismiss her feelings. Encourage her to talk to her health care provider, and remind her that, with time and treatment, she can feel better.

Most people with depression need treatment to feel better.

If you think you may have depression, start by making an appointment to see your health care provider. This could be your primary doctor or a health provider who specialises in diagnosing and treating mental health conditions (for example, a psychologist or psychiatrist). Certain medications, and some medical conditions, such as viruses or a thyroid disorder, can cause the same symptoms as depression. A health care provider can rule out these possibilities by doing a physical exam, interview, and lab tests. Your health care provider will examine you and talk to you about treatment options and next steps.

Talking to Your Health Care Provider About Your Mental Health

Communicating well with your health care provider can improve your care and help you both make good choices about your health. Read about tips to help prepare and get the most out of your visit. For additional resources, including questions to ask your health care provider, visit the Agency for Healthcare Research and Quality.

Depression can hurt—literally.

Sadness is only a small part of depression. Some people with depression do not feel sadness at all. A person with depression also may experience different physical sensations, such as muscle soreness, head pain, muscle contractions, or digestive disturbances. Someone with depression also may have trouble with sleeping, waking up in the morning, and feeling tired.

If you have been experiencing any of the following signs and symptoms for at least two weeks, you may be suffering from depression:

- Persistent sad, anxious, or "empty" mood
- Feelings of hopelessness or pessimism
- Irritability
- Feelings of guilt, worthlessness, or helplessness
- Decreased energy or fatigue
- Difficulty sleeping, early morning awakening, or oversleeping
- Loss of interest or pleasure in hobbies and activities
- Moving or talking more slowly

- Feeling restless or having trouble sitting still
- Difficulty concentrating, remembering, or making decisions
- Changes in appetite or weight
- Thoughts of death or suicide, or suicide attempts
- Aches or pains, headaches, cramps, or digestive problems without a clear physical cause that do not ease even with treatment

Talk to your health care provider about these symptoms. Be honest, clear, and concise—your provider needs to know how you feel. Your health care provider may ask when your symptoms started, what time of day they happen, how long they last, how often they occur, if they seem to be getting worse or better, and if they keep you from going out or doing your usual activities. It may help to take the time to make some notes about your symptoms before you visit your provider.

Certain types of depression are unique to women.

Pregnancy, the postpartum period, perimenopause, and the menstrual cycle are all associated with dramatic physical and hormonal changes. Certain types of depression can occur at different stages of a woman's life.

Premenstrual Dysphoric Disorder (PMDD)

Premenstrual syndrome, or PMS, refers to moodiness and irritability in the weeks before menstruation. It is quite common, and the symptoms are usually mild. But there is a less common, more severe form of PMS called premenstrual dysphoric disorder (PMDD). PMDD is a serious condition with disabling symptoms such as irritability, anger, depressed mood, sadness, suicidal thoughts, appetite changes, bloating, breast tenderness, and joint or muscle pain.

Perinatal Depression

Being pregnant isn't easy. Pregnant women commonly deal with morning sickness, weight gain, and mood swings. Caring for a newborn is challenging, too. Many new moms experience the "baby blues"—a term used to describe mild mood changes and feelings of worry, unhappiness, and exhaustion that many women sometimes experience in the first two weeks after having a baby. These feelings usually last a week or two and then go away as a new mom adjusts to having a newborn.

Perinatal depression is a mood disorder that can affect women during pregnancy and after childbirth and is much more serious than the "baby blues." The word "perinatal" refers to the time before and after the birth of a child. Perinatal depression includes depression that begins during pregnancy (called prenatal depression) and depression that begins after the baby is born (called postpartum depression). Mothers with perinatal depression experience feelings of extreme sadness, anxiety, and fatigue that may make it difficult for them to carry out daily tasks, including caring for themselves, their new child, or others.

If you think you have perinatal depression, you should talk to your health care provider or trained mental health care professional. If you see any signs of depression in a loved one during her pregnancy or after the child is born, encourage her to see a health care provider or visit a clinic.

To learn more about perinatal depression, see the National Institute of Mental Health's (NIMH) <u>Perinatal Depression brochure</u>.

Perimenopausal Depression

Perimenopause (the transition into menopause) is a normal phase in a woman's life that can sometimes be challenging. If you are going through perimenopause, you might be experiencing abnormal periods, problems sleeping, mood swings, and hot flashes. Although these symptoms are common, feeling depressed is not. If you are struggling with irritability, anxiety, sadness, or loss of enjoyment at the time of the menopause transition, you may be experiencing perimenopausal depression.

Depression affects each woman differently.

Not every woman who is depressed experiences every symptom. Some women experience only a few symptoms. Others have many. The severity and frequency of symptoms, and how long they last, will vary depending on the individual and the severity of the illness.

Depression can be treated.

Even the most severe cases of depression can be treated. Depression is commonly treated with medication, psychotherapy (also called "talk therapy"), or a combination of the two.

Antidepressants are medications commonly used to treat depression. People respond differently to antidepressants, and you may need to try different medicines to find the one that works best. Researchers also are studying and developing other medications for depression, such as brexanolone for postpartum depression, and esketamine. You can learn about recent developments on these and other medications at <u>NIMH's Science News webpage</u> under the topic "Treatments."

There are many different types of psychotherapy, such as cognitive behavioural therapy or interpersonal therapy. The particular approach a therapist uses depends on the condition being treated and the training and experience of the therapist. Therapists also may combine and adapt elements of different approaches.

Depression affects each individual differently. There is no "one-size-fits-all" for treatment. It may take some trial and error to find the treatment that works best. You can learn more about the different types of depression treatment, including psychotherapy, medication, and brain stimulation therapies, on the NIMH's webpage about <u>depression</u>. Visit the <u>Food and Drug Administration website</u> for the latest information on medication approvals, warnings, and patient information guides.

What to Consider When Looking for a Therapist

Therapists and patients work together, and finding a good match is important. The following tips can help you find the right therapist.

Ask about their areas of expertise. Therapists have different professional backgrounds and specialties. You want to find a therapist who has experience working with your specific condition.

Find out what kinds of treatments they use. Ask if those treatments are effective for dealing with your particular mental health problem or issue.

Find out how you'll evaluate progress. Determine how long treatment is expected to last, and when you should expect to gain relief from symptoms and improve your quality of life.

Don't be afraid to keep looking. Rapport and trust are essential. Discussions in therapy are deeply personal, and it's important that you feel comfortable with the therapist you pick.

This publication is in the public domain and may be reproduced or copied without permission from NIMH. <u>Citation of NIMH</u> as a source is appreciated.

U.S. DEPARTMENT OF HEALTH AND HUMAN SERVICES
National Institutes of Health
NIH Publication No. 20-MH-4779
Revised 2020

TRY Again. This
time it will work.

– GOD

www.marciampublishing.com

www.ingramcontent.com/pod-product-compliance
Lightning Source LLC
Chambersburg PA
CBRC091545030726
47636CB00017B/527